FROM CIVIL RIGHTS TO HUMAN RIGHTS AND SELF-DETERMINATION?

FROM CIVIL RIGHTS TO HUMAN RIGHTS AND SELF-DETERMINATION?

PROCEEDINGS OF THE IHRAAM CHICAGO CONFERENCE 2012

Clarity Press, Inc.

iHRAAM
International Human Rights Association of American Minorities

ISBN: 978-0-9853353-4-2
EBOOK: 978-0-9853353-5-9
In-house editor: Diana Collier Kly
Cover: R. Jordan P. Santos

Library of Congress Cataloging-in-Publication Data

From Civil Rights to Human Rights and Self-Determination (Conference) (2012 : Chicago, Ill.)
From civil rights to human rights and self-determination : proceedings of the IHRAAM Chicago conference, 2012.
pages cm
Includes bibliographical references and index.
ISBN 978-0-9853353-4-2
1. African Americans--Legal status, laws, etc.--Congresses. I. International Human Rights Association of American Minorities. II. Title.

KF4757.A5F76 2013
342.7308'73--dc23

2012044902

Clarity Press, Inc.
Ste. 469, 3277 Roswell Rd. NE
Atlanta, GA. 30305 , USA
http://www.claritypress.com

IHRAAM
101-5170 Dunster Rd., Ste. 117
Nanaimo, BC V9T 6M4
Canada
http://www.ihraam.org

A major mechanism for exposing leading African American opinion makers to the potential that international legal paradigms of internal self-determination might hold for African American collective development within the United States.

TABLE OF CONTENTS

FOREWORD

IS THE AFRICAN AMERICAN STRUGGLE HEADING IN A NEW DIRECTION?

On April 20-21, 2012, key representatives of the African American popular leadership and intelligentsia broke new ground in Chicago at the IHRAAM-sponsored conference titled FROM CIVIL RIGHTS TO HUMAN RIGHTS AND SELF-DETERMINATION? Speakers and attendees flew in from all corners—California, Georgia, Illinois, Mississippi, New York, South Carolina, Washington, DC, Virginia and Canada.

The atmosphere in the conference hall at East-West University was electrifying, as speaker after speaker added new planks to attendees' understanding of where the African American struggle had been, where it was now, and the direction it had to go to move forward. There was no disagreement from either speakers or floor on the general direction proposed by the title of the conference: that the African American struggle must now move on from civil rights to human rights and self-determination.

The panelists included former Congresswoman and 2008 Green Party Candidate for President, Cynthia McKinney; Law Professors Vernellia Randall and Carla D. Pratt; Political Science Professor and President of the National Conference of Black Political Scientists, Dr. Tyson King-Meadows; representatives of major and historic popular African American organizations, Attorney Ava Muhammad (representing Minister Louis Farrakhan and the Nation of Islam), Attorney Chokwe Lumumba (National Chairman of the New Afrikan People's Organization and a duly elected councilman from Jackson, MS), John Boyd (Founder of the National Black Farmers Association), Queen Quet, Chieftess of the Gullah-Geechee Nation; Henry English (president of Black United Fund of Illinois); Attorney Standish Willis (leading civil rights attorney having argued before the UN Inter-American Commission on Human Rights); and international law professors Francis A. Boyle and Daniel Turp (former Canadian member of parliament for the Bloc Quebecois). The Moderators for the five panels were (1) Judge Leonard Murray, (2) Mary A. Mitchell (*Chicago Sun-Times* News columnist), (3) Kamm Howard (representing N'COBRA); (4) Chicago Attorney Gregory Mitchell and (5) Atlanta Attorney Musa Dan Fodio.

The Conference opened with an introduction by Dr. Farid I. Muhammad, a member of the IHRAAM Directorate and conference chairman. He welcomed attendees, and most particularly specified how the International Human Rights Association of American Minorities (IHRAAM) viewed its role, as an international NGO in consultative status with the United Nations, in relation to the African American struggle for equality and equal status in the United States: as that of an organization devoted to providing educational and consultative services relative to the question of self-determination, as well as facilitating the access of domestic organizations to international forums and mechanisms of the UN and other intergovernmental bodies. Dr. Muhammad underlined that as an international NGO, IHRAAM clearly cannot and does not view itself as another African American leadership organization, but rather as helping to extend technical service to such bodies.

IHRAAM Chair Diana Kly then delivered a memorial address to IHRAAM Founder and Chair, Dr. Y. N. Kly, who passed away on January 6th, 2011. She outlined his long commitment to the struggle from an early age, his contribution as an engaged and award-winning scholar and writer to bringing the African American struggle to the UN, and bringing the Attention of African Americans to the usefulness and applicability of international law to their struggle.

On PANEL ONE Civil Rights: Necessary But Not Sufficient?, Cynthia McKinney, Vernellia Randall and Tyson King-Meadows took the measure of the achievements of the civil rights struggle. All were clear that despite the election of President Barack Obama and the powerful psychological impact of his presidency, little benefit was flowing to African Americans, whose economic situation overall was disproportionately worsening. Cynthia McKinney spoke passionately on the need of the African American people to get a grip on their identity as a people, and to reclaim leadership from those individuals who purport to speak for African Americans but did not achieve leadership positions due to African American support or remain unresponsive to African American needs. Vernellia Randall spoke on Dying While Black and raised the issue of recognizing the specific identity of those Black Americans whose African ancestors had been enslaved in the United States and went on to produce a new ethnic group here in America which did not look to any particular state abroad. Tyson King-Meadows projected the overall movement of the African American situation to date as moving "From Hallowed Ground to Hollowed Victories: Black Civil Rights and the Post-Racialism Imagination". The role of black elected officials was critically assessed, as was the issue of whether that elected leadership was or indeed even could be effective in addressing the needs of African Americans, and what should be done about that.

On PANEL TWO: Internal Self-determination for Historically Oppressed Peoples, Daniel Turp outlined the centuries-long struggle of the Quebecois people for self-determination, how that effort proceeded through repeated referenda until the French-speaking people of Canada were at last recognized as a Founding Nation of the multinational Canadian state, and how it was not yet achieved, were moving it closer to that goal. Ava Muhammad, recalling the longstanding commitment of the Nation of Islam to achieving African American self-determination, stressed the need for self-organization on a land base, such as was achieved by the Mormons in Utah and by the Amish, whereby the African American people might similarly be able to lay down their own structures and institutions for conducting their affairs. Carla D. Pratt pointed out how the US government's historical record of racializing group identity rather than politically determining it negatively impacted the relationship of Africans to Indians in North America, tying identity to physical characteristics and thereby setting the groundwork for both the expulsion of those Africans who had self-identified and been accepted as Indians, and for the "one-drop" blood notion of determining ethnic identity rather than the international norm of self-identification and community acceptance.

On the evening of April 20th, at the Banquet held at the Ramada Inn Lake Shore, international law professor Francis A. Boyle gave the after-dinner address, titled "African Americans' Right to Self-Determination". Dr. Boyle reviewed the findings of a Special Tribunal held in San Francisco in 1998, entitled *USA On Trial: The International Tribunal on Indigenous Peoples and Oppressed Nations in the United States*. At that time, Professor Boyle served as prosecutor before the Tribunal, presenting the African Americans' case for self-determination as resting on their historical victimization through genocide, war crimes and crimes against humanity as substantiated by the terms of the Genocide Convention and the Nuremberg Principles, and the ongoing suffering and inequalities suffered by the descendant communities of enslaved Africans as part of the lingering after-trauma effects of their historical experience. The seven impartial outside jurists brought in to adjudicate the event found this a winning argument.

On April 21, 2012, the Conference then addressed the issues to be dealt with by PANEL THREE: Collective Empowerment, Institutions, Jurisdictions, Dr. Farid I. Muhammad set the stage by presenting empirical data capturing African American attitudes toward the notion of self-determination, and the creation of a political body representing their collective interests: the findings of his IHRAAM-sponsored national telephone survey (which sampled households in 24 major, geographically diverse and predominantly African Americans cities) found that 67% of all African Americans were in favor of establishing a National Assembly while 81% were in favor of exercising more direct control over institutions in their local communities. Chokwe Lumumba, from his vantage point of decades of leadership of the Republic of New Afrika and now as councilman in Jackson, Mississippi, stressed the importance of land and economic development to the achievement of self-determination, spoke to the establishment of the developing Kush Region in Mississippi, and invited African Americans to return to their historical homelands in the South. John Boyd, as leader of the 100,000 strong movement of Black farmers, also addressed the importance of land, not just as politically-governed territory, but for the anchoring of traditions and self worth for the family and the soul, and how it is the ultimate resource for sustenance in times of need. Henry English emphasized the need for self-reliance, and indicated how the Black United Fund of Illinois had been able to support a variety of community projects through their membership-driven fund. He pointed out how African Americans need to approach their issues as a group, since America has been a country of groups since it was founded, and that unity is the key to their situation

On PANEL FOUR: USING THE UN TO ADVANCE AFRICAN AMERICAN INTERESTS, Attorney Standish Willis advised how he had successfully accessed the Inter-American Commission on Human Rights concerning the torture of African American prisoners, and brought direct pressure to bear on the American government through the state reporting requirements of the Convention for the Elimination of All Forms of Discrimination (CERD). Queen Quet of the Gullah-Geechee Nation took to the dais singing, with the flag of the Gullah-Geechee Nation attached to the speaker's podium. She advised how through IHRAAM's facilitation, she had been the first to officially address the United Nations in Gullah, as a representative of her people, had been engaged with UNESCO and the UN Forum on Minority Rights, how the US government had recognized the existence of the Gullah-Geechees through the establishment of the Gullah-Geechee Heritage Corridor, and had been granted (as international law professor Francis Boyle affirmed from the floor) de facto recognition by the US government. She indicated that the Gullah-Geechee nation had a constitution, and a legislative body, with other instruments of governance being projected. Atty. Dan Fodio called from the floor that the Gullah-Geechee Nation represented a microcosm that might well inform African Americans as they pursue their own struggle.

The much-anticipated PANEL FIVE: WHAT NEXT? could not be fully addressed due to time constraints. However, the essence of what needed to be done had clearly emerged through the discussions that took place in the question and answer sessions that followed each panel, and the quality ongoing exchanges among speakers themselves. The problematic issues concerned how to recapture African American leadership from those who had been placed into leadership positions by others, as well as how to address the varied psycho-historical issues and challenges of identity uniquely experienced by formerly-enslaved peoples of African Descent in the United States. Finally, the need for a political body speaking directly and specifically to the needs of African Americans (a Constituent Assembly) was raised and was received so positively that it seemed as if it were a foregone conclusion. All speakers agreed that while international law and custom might provide guidance and legitimacy for the African American struggle and a forum in which to pursue it, there was no substitute for self-organization, self-reliance and true self-determination. It was recognized by all that this protracted struggle would have to be waged family by family, block by block, city by city and ultimately state by state. It was recognized that true self-determination for African-Americans wouldn't be won overnight, but was a process of continued engagement that could be the mission of future generations.

A video of the conference is available for circulation and showing by other interested African American organizations, as well as on YouTube.

From left to right: Atty. Musa Dan Fodio, Dr. Tyson King-Meadows, Diana Collier Kly, Cynthia McKinney, Judge Leonard Murray, Dr. Farid I. Muhammad

OPENING ADDRESS

FARID I. MUHAMMAD

Greetings everyone. My name is Farid Muhammad. I serve as Chairman of the Department of Behavioral Sciences here at East-West University (EWU) and have the distinct privilege of being a member of the Directorate of the International Human Rights Association of American Minorities (IHRAAM). As you might well know, IHRAAM is an international NGO in Consultative Status with the United Nations.

On behalf of my distinguished colleagues and fellow members of the Directorate of IHRAAM, as well as the central administration of EWU which has been gracious enough to make this venue available to us. We would like to welcome our distinguished panelists, moderators and audience to this unique two-day conference titled "From Civil Rights to Human Rights & Self-Determination?"

We trust that the dialogue initiated during this conference will lead to even further discussion and hopefully pragmatic attempts to address the many challenging issues that might surface. In a few minutes, I will defer to my dear colleague—Mrs. Diana Kly—Acting Chairperson of the IHRAAM Directorate and wife of its Founder, the late Dr. Y. N. Kly, to provide you with more intimate insight into the personal life and character of this truly historic figure.

First, let me begin by extending a personal note of thanks to both the Chancellor (Dr. Khan) and Provost (Dr. Jain) of EWU and for allowing us to use this auditorium, the adjoining facilities and equipment. We sincerely appreciate this most gracious gesture of support. It is appropriate to mention that EWU is a non-profit and non-sectarian institution of higher learning. It serves a student body that is quite diverse in age, ethnic backgrounds, economic circumstances and academic preparation. We serve approximately a thousand students with a student body that is roughly 70% African-American, 11% Hispanic, and we have additional student representation from every major domestic and foreign-born ethnic, cultural and linguistic community. Over half of our students are first time members of their families to attend a university. As you might come to note during your stay with us, we have just begun construction on a new 17-storey building which will accommodate dormitory facilities, on Wabash Avenue.

It is obvious from the central theme of this conference that we hope to address what are perhaps complex, not well-understood or well-appreciated geo-political issues. Hopefully, we will come to better understand, no doubt by way of the central topics to be addressed by our distinguished panelists—that there are conceptual, political and more specifically domestic/international legal implications in the attempt to juxtapose "Civil Rights", "Human Rights", and "Self-determination".

Needless to say, there is an additional challenge in one's attempt to apply these now universally accepted legal themes to the plight of peoples of African Descent throughout the world diaspora—and now with micro-level application to the African-American Community here in the United States. In our attempt to do so, it might behoove us to first appreciate the full global or macro-level challenges that confront all humankind.

If we could reduce the world's population, which now exceeds 7 billion, to a village or this auditorium of 100 people, with all existing human ratios remaining the same, the demographics would look something like this:

60 of us would be Asian
14 of us would be African
12 of us would be European
8 of us Latin Americans
5 of us Americans and Canadians who would control
32% of the entire world's wealth
49 of us would be female
51 would be male
82 would be non-white
18 would be white
Half of us would be under 24 years of age
80 would live in substandard housing
67 would be unable to read
50 would be malnourished and 1 dying of starvation
33 would not have access to safe water supply

1 would have HIV
1 would be near death
2 would be near birth
20 would live on less than US$1.00 a day
48 would live on less than US$2.00 a day
Only 1 would have a college education

Threfore, if one were to take a look at the world from this condensed perspective, the need for international cooperation, understanding, education, self-reliance and mutual respect among both nations and peoples could not be more self-evident.

Thematic to concerns that particularly impact peoples of African descent who, for reasons that are historically well-documented, suffer disproportionately relative to all major socio-economic indicators of well-being... The UN attempts to address the problem of multi-ethnic states and the protection of minority rights.

In its summary of the internationally accepted declarations following the historic World Conference Against Racism held in Durban, South African in 2001, the UN has stated the following:

> In today's world, multi-ethnic states are the norm. The traditional nation-state, where a distinct national group corresponds to a territorial unit, has become an endangered species. Globalization and the increasing movement of people across borders threaten to kill off the nation-state once and for all. However, some myths resist reality, and majority or dominant cultures in countries around the world seek to impose their identity on other groups with whom they share a territory.
>
> Attempts to impose uniculturalism in multi-ethnic environments often come at the expense of minority rights. To avoid marginalization, minorities often intensify their efforts to preserve and protect their identity. The hardening of opposing forces—assimilation on the one hand and preservation of minority identity on the other—can cause increased intolerance and, in the worst case, armed ethnic conflict. In such cases and in order to prevent escalation, the protection and promotion of minority rights becomes essential. [UN—WCAR Declaration]

In 1992 and subsequent to the international ratification of other major human rights covenants, the UN General Assembly adopted the Declaration on the Rights of Persons Belonging to National or Ethnic, Religious and Linguistic Minorities. Multilateral monitoring of the compliance of states to their international commitments with regard to protecting minority rights has increased transparency.

The formation of an international Working Group on Minorities and more recently a UN Working Group on Peoples of African Descent, are all part of the evolving international instrumentation that can and should be brought to bear in any comprehensive attempt to address the collective concerns of peoples of African descent in general and African Americans in particular.

The foregoing hopefully provides us with another conceptual paradigm by which and through which we might now consider the unique socio-political and economic problematic of African Americans in the USA. Contemporary forms of racism, racial discrimination, xenophobia and related intolerance in both the US and elsewhere continue to mount. As is well evidenced by way of both governmental and non-governmental sources of research, gross disparities between the majority ethny and the African American community relative to such critical socio-economic indicators as: health, education, employment, political participation, economic development, criminal justice and the application of the death penalty, police violence and incitement to racial hatred are well documented and continue to worsen.

The summary of one such study by the PEW Research Center released in July 2011 titled "Wealth Gaps Rise to Record Highs Bewteen Whites, Blacks & Hispanics" helps drive this point home. This study revealed that "The median wealth of white households is 20 times that of Black households and 18 times that of Hispanitc households." The PEW Research analysis found that, in percentage terms, the bursting of the housing market bubble in 2006 and the recession that followed from late 2007 to mid-2009 took a far greater told on the wealth of minorities than whites. From 2005 to 2009, inflation-adjusted median wealth fell by 16% for whites but a phenomenal 53% for African Americans.

In 2005 the median net worth of households for whites was \$132,992—for African Americans it was just \$12,124. By 2009 the median net worth of households for whites decreased 16% to \$113,149 while African American households lost a resounding 53% of their total net worth and went from \$12,124 in 2005 to \$5,677 by 2009.

I merely note this one empirical indicator of social well being where such systemic disparities exist. While we do not want to dwell in the past, make excuses and/or simply find fault in ourselves or others, we do sincerely pray that the themes addressed by the four panels in this 2-day conference, will help provide further insight and perhaps new strategies for the resolution of the collective and legitimate concerns of American minorities.

In conclusion, it is important to note what IHRAAM is and is not. IHRAAM should not be viewed as just another organization contending for leadership in the African American struggle. Nor are we apologists for the United Nations. Instead, as an NGO, IHRAAM's role is to help provide facilitation, education and consultation, particularly for those aggrieved groups needing specialized access to the social, political and legal protection afforded them under international law. Respectfully, African Americans are one of many such struggling groups in this hemisphere and elsewhere.

We hope that the questions raised and which require due consideration will help provoke the creation of a new paradigm of collective thought and action that can move the African American community toward legitimate expression of self-determination and the ultimate achievement of equal status with all Americans.

Distinguished guests, as we now conclude this introductory and memorial phase of today's proceedings, it is now my privilege and honor to introduce to you the wife of the late Dr. Y. N. Kly, who was the founder and chairman of the IHRAAM Directorate. As you will note in both the Memorial Display and the brief biography distributed to you with your conference program, Dr. Kly was awarded the title of Professor Emeritus by the School of Human Justice at the university of Regina in Canada where he taught international law and human justice.

His publications and awards are too numerous to mention in this context and are noted elsewhere in the auditorium. More importantly—as far as I am personally concerned—he was a true and dear friend and colleague who will be sorely missed. He was a brilliant, honorable and decent man. His true and lasting contribution to his community and world society at large is still a work in progress. At the conclusion of the remarks made by Mrs. Kly, we will ask for a brief moment of silence in memory of our dear friend. Following her remarks, anyone so inclined will be allowed a brief moment to make a comment if they so choose.

Now it is my distinct honor to introduce Mrs. Diana Collier Kly. In addition to her being a Chief Communications Officer and Policy Consultant for IHRAAM over the years, she is also a well-noted Publisher and business person in her own right. She is also Editorial Director of Clarity Press, Inc., an independent publisher on global issues and alternatives. So without any further ado, it is my pleasure to introduce to you a dear friend and colleague, Mrs. Diana Collier Kly.

HONORING IHRAAM FOUNDER DR. Y. N. KLY

I'm very grateful to have this opportunity to speak to you about the lifelong work and engagement in the African American struggle of my husband, Dr. Yussuf Naim Kly. Indeed, it may be that the time has come at last for the thoughtful examination and discussion of those ideas to which he dedicated his life. Paradoxically it comes not just at a time when the people of the United States of America have put a black President into the highest office of the land, but at a time when African Americans have had an opportunity to measure how well that has played out on their behalf, to assess the fruits along with—not the failures, but the insufficiencies—of the Civil Rights struggle of which this election represents the crowning achievement.

Indeed, as the Civil Rights struggle has demonstrated, groundbreaking systemic changes are possible in the United States that effectively undo one institutionalization of the relations between whites and blacks, and put another in its place. What a momentous change that brought about since 1935 when Dr. Kly was born in the state of South Carolina. Back then, the descendants of diverse African peoples were still subjected to the American version of apartheid called segregation. Dr. Kly was born two decades before the civil rights struggle was to begin, though as his later book, *The Invisible War: The African American Anti-Slavery Resistance from the Stono Rebellion through the Seminole Wars* would demonstrate, the enslaved Africans had always struggled against the institutions of slavery, a struggle that the victors have hidden in their histories by calling that resistance the Seminole Wars.

Dr. Kly grew up in a poor neighborhood of Columbia. His father was a barber. His mother wrote books, and would go on to become one of the early recognized African American writers in the state. Dr. Kly's sister Doris told me that from the very beginning, he seemed to have a sense of purpose. So it was hardly surprising to anybody, she said, that after high school he headed straight off for college at South Carolina State. Then she told me how shocked everybody was when, six days after they packed him off, his luggage was right back there on the front porch. What could conceivably have gone wrong...? Had he quit?

Dr. Kly told his family that since they weren't going to teach him what he needed to know at that college, he was done with it. You might recall that during the apartheid period in South Carolina, African Americans were not permitted to study political science. Not that he was going to give up, no. But, he told them, he was going to go somewhere else where they would teach him what he needed to learn. If his family would just give him $100 to do so, then he would never ask them for anything again. And that is what they did.

It took two decades, but by 1975, Dr. Kly had a doctorate in Political Science, with a specialty in international human rights law from the very excellent Laval University in Quebec City, Canada. His thesis was titled "International Law and the Black Minority in the United States". It was later published and positively reviewed in the American flagship journal, *The American Journal of International Law*. I want to read you an excerpt from that review, because it sets out what we are trying to talk about today:

> Kly's strategic placement of the US view of the collective rights of its minorities within the more widely accepted normative discourse of international law provides not only an alternative vision of race relations in the United States, but also, even more importantly, an alternative solution. Kly's unique perspective is worthy of consideration and debate by minority and non-minority individuals alike.

But even though he now had a doctorate and it was the heyday of affirmative action, Dr. Kly couldn't get a job in the United States teaching political science and international law, and more particularly not on the groundbreaking findings of his thesis. After getting his doctorate, the only contract he could get at an American university was here at Chicago State University some thirteen years later—for a few sessions lecturing on Plato and Kant that would not lead to full time employment. It was 1988, we were living in Hyde Park and our son, Sundiata, had just been born at the University of Chicago hospital. We were forced to return to Canada. But before leaving Chicago, Dr. Kly founded the International Human Rights Association of American Minorities (IHRAAM) with the help of Chicago activists Bob White, Tele E'mani and Dr. Farid Muhammad. The theoretical foundations of IHRAAM had cemented during discussions with Dr. Charles Knox and Dr. Yvonne King during the attendance of all three at The Hague Academy of International Law in 1983. Knox and King were former members of the Black Panther Party, who had gone on to found the NCBL Community College of Law and International Diplomacy, the first African American founded and supported educational institution of its ilk in America.

The thinking was that there was a need to internationalize the African American struggle, as Malcolm X had called for. But for the IHRAAM founders that meant not only to draw world attention to the oppression of African Americans in America, not only to take their case to the United Nations, but also to promote among African Americans an understanding of international legal norms and customary state practice with regard to how minority/majority relations are constitutionally institutionalized in order for African Americans to achieve an equal-status relationship, not just individually but collectively, with white Americans. At the UN, other states and other minorities understood that kind of a dilemma: how the special needs of a smaller people—to say nothing of an historically oppressed people--can be pushed aside or determined by the dominant group in the electoral platforms and political processes the state, in its governing institutions, in its policy formation, and in the implementation of laws when the way all of that is set up has been dominated and controlled by the majority and reflects their interests, their concerns and their particular ways of doing things.

At as an international NGO in consultative status at the UN, under Dr. Kly's guidance, IHRAAM would go on to make alliances with similar groups facing similar issues. This would lead to two historic international conferences held by IHRAAM in Geneva on the United Nations and the Right to Self-Determination, one in 2000 and the second in 2004. They were participated in by representatives of oppressed internal nations from all over the world – not just peoples encompassed within the borders or the legal system of the United States, such as Native Americans, Puerto Ricans, Kanaka Maoli, Gullah Geechees, but other peoples similarly entrapped within other multinational states, such as the Dalits and Kashmiris in India, the Quebecois and First Nations in Canada, the Irish Catholics, Tamils, Zanzibaris, Sami, and so on.

But I jump ahead of the chronology here. Let me go back.

Even while living in exile in Canada, where by 1989 he finally had secured a full time position teaching human rights and international law at the University of Regina, Dr. Kly remained immersed in the African American struggle. In 1991, he took the LAPD beating of Rodney King to the United Nations under UN Special Procedure 1503, a mechanism for addressing complaints about "situations which appear to reveal a consistent pattern of gross and reliably attested violations of human rights" in a country. It was historic, it was what Malcolm X had called for. It was the first time that the African American situation had been formally presented to the United Nations via a UN mechanism, voiced in international legal terms, and based on international treaties to which the US was a signatory—as opposed to protesting with signs on the street outside the UN, or at a local church. The Petition caused a great stir at the time, and came very close to the US being listed for official UN investigation. So Dr. Kly was informed by one of the US representatives then on the Sub-Commission.

Dr. Kly also pursued other UN initiatives, in particular contributing to the Working Group that was then drafting what would become the UN Declaration on the Rights of National or Ethnic, Religious and Linguistic Minorities. In reflection of these efforts, in 1993 IHRAAM was awarded Consultative Status with the UN.

He also continued to write. Two of these books, his very first book mentioned earlier, and *A Popular Guide to Minority Rights,* went on to win the prestigious OUTSTANDING BOOK Award from the Gustavus Center for the Study of Human Rights in 1990 and 1995. But he still couldn't get hired as a professor of political science in the United States, even so.

Over the years, Dr. Kly tried to make both the popular leadership of African Americans and the oppression African Americans faced in the United States visible on this international stage. He wanted the popular African American leadership to learn from the experience of other peoples in the world, to recognize their dilemma here in the United States of America as reflecting not unique problems, but rather normal problems that numerically smaller historically disadvantaged peoples face when they are incorporated into a larger multinational state run by and in the interest of a dominant cultural majority. Dr. Kly inspired and assisted many other African American organizations to proceed in this direction, to gain this scope, to the extent that in 2007 the National Bar Association's International Law Section gave him its Lifetime Achievement Award for pioneering work in the introduction of international law to the African American community.

Dr. Kly also worked tirelessly on behalf of many other minority groups and indigenous and unrepresented nations, winning their love and respect. Just before I attended the Memorial Luncheon held at the Palais des Nations for Dr. Kly (which paradoxically was attended by the

US Ambassador to the UN in Geneva), I received a phone call from Rudy James, First Raven of the Alaskan Thling'it Nation, who told me to tell them—and I did—how the Native nations revered him for all the work he had done on their behalf. In 2007, as an instance,

Dr. Kly submitted a Petition on behalf of the Lil'wat Indigenous Nation to the Organization of American States' regional court. It was a complex case, and Dr. Kly had very deftly interwoven the issues of individual rights with those of the right of indigenous nations to self-determination, but as the years passed, we started to think they had shelved it. it wasn't until 2011, after Dr. Kly's death, that the Inter-American Commission on Human Rights advised IHRAAM that it had given the state of Canada one month to respond to the Lil'wat Petition. Canada replied with some 20 pages and 10 attachments; IHRAAM countered that, and the Court has now put the matter back in Canada's court once again, where it presently stands.

But this wasn't the most extreme instance of Dr. Kly's work bearing fruit years later. When we went to India in 2009 seeking medical treatment for Dr. Kly, the trip was paid for by the International Council for Human Rights, an allied organization concerned with the struggle human rights in Kashmir, we learned when we arrived that Dr. Kly's writing on International Law and the Dalits, written back at least a decade earlier, was just being published by a University Law School in New Delhi; the book launch was that very week.

I mention this to illustrate another important factor as it relates to social change: that just as huge systemic changes such as the dismantlement of apartheid can take place in a relatively swift period of time, so too can initiatives that began many years earlier go on to bear fruit much later in the future.

Throughout his lifetime, Dr. Kly kept trying to return to the United States but he was unable to do so. Nonetheless, he remained an engaged scholar devoted to furthering the African American struggle over all those years, writing books to try to guide it. These were not protest books, not histories, but books that sought to elucidate a roadmap forward for the African American people, the kind of direction that now, as a political scientist and a specialist in international minority rights law, Dr. Kly had set out to find when just a young man with $100 in his pocket, who had decided to leave all he knew in search of it.

In 2010, while he was dying, Dr. Kly wrote *The Black Book II: The True Problematic of African American Liberation.* And what was the nub of the issue that he told me to be sure to pass on to you? Suffice it to say for now that Dr. Kly wanted you to know this: if you, as African Americans, decide that you not only share a common past, but also seek a collective future as a united people living and working together in your own communities here in America—that this is your right, that this is normal, that African Americans don't have to change to be like somebody else (whether Africans or Anglo Americans), they don't have to be sprinkled among other peoples as if there was some kind of a problem every time there was ... just us ... and that African Americans' right to instrumentalize a common future here in the United States is enshrined in international law and can be demonstrated in actuality in the best practices of other states as models and examples of how it can be done.

And this is what we hope to just begin to explore, here today.

Diana Collier Kly
April 20, 2012

PANEL ONE

CIVIL RIGHTS: NECESSARY BUT NOT SUFFICIENT?

- Did the civil rights struggle reach its peak with the election of a Black President?
- Are civil rights sufficient to ensure African-Americans equality in social well being indicators such as health, employment, income, education, home ownership, etc?
- What are African-Americans' international rights under the Convention on the Elimination of All Forms of Racial Discrimination (CERD)?
- Has US policy fulfilled these rights and obligations?
- What is the current status of special measures (affirmative action) in the US, as required by CERD and other relevant international Human Rights instruments?

Left to Right: Speakers Prof. Vernellia Randall, Dr. Tyson King-Meadows, Cynthia McKinney, and moderator, Judge Leonard Murray

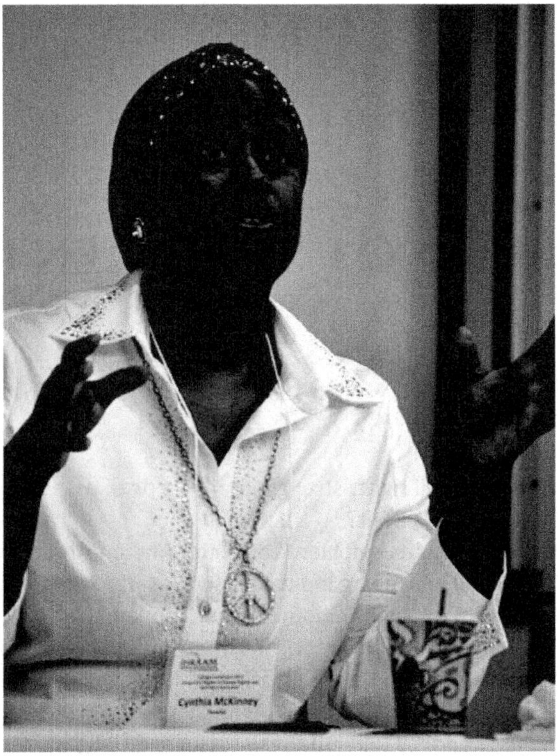

CYNTHIA McKINNEY was the first African American woman to represent Georgia in the United States House of Representatives, where she supported the creation of a Palestinian State in the Israel-occupied territory, sparked controversy by criticizing American policy in the Middle East, and criticized the U.S. government's response to Hurricane Katrina. After serving 6 terms in the House, in 2007, she left the Democratic Party and became the Green Party Presidential Candidate for President in 2008. Cynthia is a vocal advocate of the creation of peaceful US foreign policy. She joined the Bike4Peace 2010 cyclists, and completed a 21-city peace tour in the United States educating urban communities in order to promote a more peaceful U.S. foreign policy. She is a supporter and follower of Tun Dr. Mahathir Mohamad's efforts to "criminalize war", and served as an official observer at the historic Kuala Lumpur War Crimes Tribunal that found former President George W. Bush and former Prime Minister Tony Blair guilty of the crime of aggression and other crimes against the state and people of Iraq. She is editor of *The Illegal War on Libya* and (forthcoming) *Ain't Nothing Like Freedom.* McKinney holds a B.A. in international relations from the University of Southern California, and an M.A. in Law and Diplomacy from the Fletcher School of Law and Diplomacy.

UNDERSTANDING WHO YOU ARE

Cynthia McKinney

Whether it is civil rights or human rights, if you do not know who you are, then you will not fight for what you deserve. And, what we have sustained in this country is an attack on our identity, at its very core. I am not a lawyer like Vernellia Randall, so maybe she can correct me, but when civil rights, human rights, self-determination are denied, that is one thing. When identity is denied, that is equivalent to genocide. So that is where I will start.

I wanted to talk about my two favorite speeches that I have written. I get into trouble because I love to write and I have these ideas and when I start to write they start to flow. The first speech goes to this idea of identity which is critical for us to launch a struggle for self-determination. The name of the speech is "Which Way Will You Go When the Conductor Calls?" And that speech comes from my great grandmother who could pass for white. So she would get on the segregated train and the conductor would direct her this way, the way for white people to go, but she had in tow my father, and my father could not pass for white, and so, rather than escape who she was into a life that was unimaginable, she understood who she was; she understood her identity, and she went to the colored car. So despite the conductors call, she went with who she was. But even more than that, what she did was, as pale as she was, she would sit in the chair and cross her legs. I'm little. I would sit in the crook between her ankle and her foot, and I would ride up and down on her leg. And she would say to me, "Gal, be proud of your color." I got that from age 3, age 4, age 5, age 6. "Gal, be proud of your color." So identity for me was instilled in me from my very first conscious moments.

My second most favorite speech is called, "Street Lights". And in that speech, I talk about what life in the black community was like under the street lights. Because those who are so young, you may not get it, the world's problems would be solved underneath the street lights. The street light was where everyone gathered when it was dark, and there were kids that would play with junebugs, and some men shooting dice, and other men that were solving the community's problems and talking about black people.They were having fun, some talking about their exploits, but there was life seething under the street lights.

I gave this speech in front of the African Administrators of Transportation, because under Bill Clinton the Secretary of Transportation was a black man, Rodney Slater, and Rodney Slater held a conference for African Administrators of Transportation in Atlanta. I was there, and I gave this speech. That speech was a labor of love. In that speech I say that for one week in the United States there was nothing happening under the street lights. What in the world could bring life to a halt under the street lights? What was it? Reports said crime went down for one week. And what it was,was *Roots* was on. And black people in this country vicariously were able to transport themselves into an identity. We could find out where we came from and who we were, what our original language was. Every fourth grade child has this homework assignment, "My Immigrant Roots". So the child has to trace back to where their ancestors came from. Well I ripped my child's teacher a new one when he brought that paper home, because I thought it was insensitive because I do not know where I come from, I do not know what my roots are. And so, for that one week we all knew where we came from. And could walk with a difference step, we could talk with a different lyricism in our voices, because we had some idea of who we were.

So here's where I think our problem exists today. There's a scene in *Roots*, for me, which is the most powerful scene, when Kunta Kinte gets "broken" and he is forced to assume the ID of Toby. Now enough people in the audience knew there was an opportunity for the 44th anniversary for NBC to play *Roots* on television again, but they refused. They do not want you to know that history, they do not want you to know your identity—so they can tell you, you are Toby or worse.

And this is what I want to say about that scene, because the players in that scene include the plantation owner. The plantation owner is upset because Kunta Kinte has not been broken yet. The other person is Fiddler, the black man that was supposed to tame Kunta Kinte. And

Fiddler did not do his job. Kunta Kinte has run away again and he got caught. He kept running away and running away. "He was a bad example for the other slaves," the plantation owner says. So Fiddler gets replaced by a white slave driver.That white slave driver tells the black man with a lash to go get Kunta Kinte and tie him up and hang him up, suspend him from the rope. The black man does that. There is the audience of black slaves. There are 7 characters in this scene. The white plantation owner asks Kunta Kinte to tell him his name, and Kunta Kinte says, "Kunta Kinte". And the white slave driver tells the black man with the lash to whip him. And the black man whips him, and whips him, and whips him. Then the white slave driver asks, "What's your name and Kunta Kinte says, "Kunta Kinte". Then the black lash holder whips him, and whips him, and whips him again. And then again and again, he is whipped because he says that his name is Kunta Kinte. Then finally, when he is near death he says, "Toby". Then the white slaver driver tells the black man with the lash to let him down. Then Kunta Kinte is told to say it louder. By this time all the remaining slaves on the plantation have been brought out to witness the breaking of Kunta Kinte.

In our community today we got Tobys and we got fewer and fewer Kunta Kintes. Kunta Kinte is an endangered species in our community. We got the man with the lash in his hand, whipping us, and we think that he is our leader.

Ultimately, this boils down to identity. Because if you don't know, if you can't discern, Kunta Kinte from the man with the lash, then you will never get to the point of self-determination.

Much has been made around the edges of President Obama's rise and tenure in the White House about the issue of race in this country. Sadly, nothing has been made of the public policy exigencies that arise because of the urgent racial disparities that continue to plague Black people, Latinos, and Native Americans in the United States.

The world community is engaged on this issue of human rights now because the Obama Administration and the Bush and Clinton Administrations before, have used human rights as a fig leaf to obscure the conduct of more wars and war crimes that kill people.

The U.S. avoids the right of return for Palestinians as assiduously as it does for Hurricane Katrina survivors. Author Bill Quigley writes in "The Cleansing of New Orleans," that half of the working poor, elderly, and disabled of New Orleans have not been able to return. The United Nations Special Rapporteurs called for an immediate end of public housing demolitions in New Orleans. The Committee on the Elimination of Racial Discrimination, ratified by the U.S. in 1994, further observes that the U.S. must do more to protect and support the African American community. In 2006, the United Nations Human Rights Commission "noted its concern that while African Americans constitute just 12% of the population, they represent 50% of homeless people, and the government is required to take 'adequate and adequately implemented' measures to remedy this human rights violation." In short, the United Nations has issued reports squarely calling for the United States to do more to eliminate racial discrimination—and this discrimination is a human rights violation. So what are we prepared to do about it?

The reports of human rights violations in the United States are the story of you and me.

Therefore, I am deeply offended that in the middle of a Presidential campaign, no mention whatsoever is made of the deep racial disparities that communities in this country are forced to endure on a daily basis. The press demean those who thoughtfully speak of race and avoid any discussion that could illuminate the glaring racial disparities of today.

Myriad reports and studies that have been done all come up with the same basic conclusion: in order to resolve deep and persisting racial disparities in this country, a public policy initiative is urgently needed. And in order to arrive at that public policy initiative and consensus, a real discussion of race, is needed. A Harvard University/ Kaiser Family Foundation study found that there is basic ignorance in the White community of the many ways in which Black life in this country is significantly different than theirs. This points to the de facto segregation that exists in this country despite U.S. apartheid's end.

In the context of a Presidential election, there ought to be a discussion of the various public policy initiatives offered by the various candidates that will eliminate all forms and vestiges of racial discrimination, especially the racial disparities that cloud the hopes, dreams, and futures of millions of Americans.

Now, what are these disparities of which I speak?

Every year on the anniversary of the birth of Dr. Martin Luther King, Jr.United for a Fair Economy publishes a study of the true state of people of color in America called the "State of the Dream Report." And it was their 2004 report that noted that without a public policy intervention, it would take 1,664 years to close the racial gap in home ownership in this country. And that on some indices, for example, infant mortality, the racial disparities were worse in 2004 than at the time of the murder of Dr. Martin Luther King, Jr. in 1968.

Now, do you think the home ownership gap has widened, remained the same, or improved?

In their 2005 report, entitled, "Disowned," United for a Fair Economy explored the disparate impact of Bush's "Ownership Society" economic program that saw Black and Latino lives shattered as unemployment, income, home ownership, business ownership, and stock ownership plummeted even in the face of Administration economists trumpeting the phenomenal "growth" of the U.S. economy as a result of their policies.

In 2006, United for a Fair Economy focused on the devastating and embarrassing effect of government inaction before, during, and after Hurricanes Katrina and Rita. They focused on something as simple as car ownership and the relationship between vehicle ownership and race. In the case of New Orleans, car ownership literally meant the difference between losing or saving one's life.

In 2007, United for a Fair Economy explored the Black voters' attachment to the Democratic Party, and in a piece entitled, "Voting Blue, but Staying in the Red," they explored goals that the Democratic Party should have put at the top of its agenda for its first 100 hours in the majority. While noting that the Democrats didn't even mention Katrina in their agenda, United for a Fair Economy concluded that Blacks and Latinos voted in the November 2006 elections in the blue, but due to a failure of public policy that pays attention to their needs, they continued to live "in the red."

In its 2008 report, United for a Fair Economy explored the sub-prime mortgage crisis and noted that the largest loss of wealth in U.S. history was experienced by the Black and Latino communities with an estimated $92 billion lost by Blacks and an estimated $98 billion lost by Latinos. And while families are losing their life savings and the only major investment that they own, policy makers are asking them to tighten their belts while the predator banks' CEOs walk away with record remuneration.

During the Obama years, United for a Fair Economy found that Blacks were in a depression, rejected any notion of the pursuit of "colorblind" policies as a remedy because the impact of such policies was not colorblind and the Black community in particular was left drained with its dreams foreclosed. Last year, United for a Fair Economy found that if the agenda of cutting taxes and shrinking the size of government actually becomes policy, then "Dr. King's dream of a racially equal society will be pushed even further out of reach."

Sadly, United for a Fair Economy isn't the only research organization to find glaring and intolerable disparities in our society by race and no appropriate public policies enacted to address them. Hull House did a study that found that it would take 200 years to close the gap in the quality of life experienced by black Chicagoans and white Chicagoans.

Despite a Democratic mayor of Chicago and Illinois governor, there still is no public policy initiative to begin closing that gap.

Dr. David Satcher found that over 80,000 Blacks die unnecessarily and prematurely each year because of the disparate treatment Blacks receive AFTER they reach the doctor's office.

Several years ago, *The New York Times* published a finding that nearly half the men between the ages of 16 and 64 in New York City were unemployed. That was before the so-called economic crisis of today. To date, there is no initiative by the mayor or the governor of New York to begin addressing this pain.

I have two more examples of what life is really like for us inside the U.S. and then I'll get to what we—no—you—must do to arrest this: The National Urban League and Michelle Alexander's pathbreaking work.

Every year, the National Urban League publishes a study, "The State of Black America," in which the ills and disparities that persist in this country are catalogued. Every year, the story is basically the same. The United States still has a long way to go that only public policy can address.

Michelle Alexander, author of *The New Jim Crow* tells us what informs current U.S. policy. She said, "Slavery ended, but the idea of race lived on." In addition to informing us that there are more Black men in the criminal system that the U.S. has for administering justice than there were enslaved in 1864, she also says, "the criminal justice system was strategically employed to force African Americans back into a system of extreme repression and control, a tactic that would continue to prove successful for generations to come."

So, now, I hope I've sufficiently painted a picture for you that whatever it is that Black folks have been doing in the policy arena since 1978, it isn't enough—Black resident at 1600 Pennsylvania Avenue, aside. There has not been a sufficient, coordinated, mobilized Black rejoinder to the devastating facts of Black life in the U.S. and the Supreme Court decisions that have set the framework within which Black quality of life is regulated: Supreme Court decisions like *Bakke* (1978), *Croson* (1989), *Fordice* (1992), *Adarand* (1995), *Gratz* (2003), and *Fisher* (involving University of Texas admissions) that will be decided this Session. In short, the school to prison pipeline is real and exists by design while the tablecloth of programs that educated me and provided access to equal opportunity for my generation is being snatched from you while the settings remain neatly arranged on the table.

It is up to us to see what is missing and to do our best to provide for our community. That won't happen by trying to assimilate into a value structure that is alienating us. That can only happen by knowing who we are and what it is we stand for. That can only happen by mobilizing every one of us no matter where we are in the structure, but all working toward the same goal: equal treatment for all and equal opportunity for all.

U.S. society is structured as it is because the purposes of those who structured it are being served. When we dare to change that structure, we dare to have it respond to our needs. And I will posit this to you now: by acting to save ourselves from the way things are currently, we will also liberate the global community because our values are not to step on the dreams of anyone.

So, what do I mean by this?

In short, what I'm trying to say is that things will only get worse if we do nothing. The people in charge of things have demonstrated that they will not be satisfied until they've stolen every house, clearcut every forest, subjugated every people, and destroyed every nation. Doing nothing ensures that things will only get worse for us and the world.

Meanwhile, if change is really what you want, you'll have to be willing to work and sacrifice for it. Those who created this structure will offer you a celebrity of immense wealth here, a CEO there, maybe even the Presidency, itself—if you choose to become a part of—a perpetrator in—their structure of injustice. They will offer you scholarships to their schools and will stamp you with their imprimatur if you promise to do nothing to improve the lot of others, they'll even allow you to become a Member of Congress or a professor at one of their beloved institutions—that is if you commit to being a bystander to injustice, remaining silent on the things that really matter. But the only way to change the results of next year's United for a Fair Economy report—or the National Urban League's State of Black America report—or any other report about race in this country, is for you to choose the path that I have chosen—to become a courageous resister to injustice. To wake up every morning and say to yourself, what am I going to do to resist today? What am I going to do today to mess up their plan to marginalize, alienate, and kill? This means that courageous resisters can exist in every segment of society. No matter where they find themselves, courageous resisters know their charge.

Sadly, we Black people tolerate and even celebrate the too many who made the Faustian bargain to become perpetrators or bystanders while we fail to even recognize the few who have chosen to take up the mantle of courageous resistance for truth, justice, peace, and dignity.

Bob Marley asked, "How long shall they kill our prophets while we stand aside and look?"

I am proud to say that while I was in Congress, I was a courageous resister:

- I voted against every Pentagon budget that came before me.
- I introduced legislation to eliminate the use of depleted uranium and to stop the transfer of U.S. weapons to regimes that did not respect human rights.

- I drafted legislation to ban the importation into the United States of coltan from the Democratic Republic of Congo.
- I represented the Congressional Black Caucus at the Durban World Conference Against Racism, and submitted a report to the UN on the COINTELPRO-inspired murders of Black Panther Party members.
- I used my Congressional perch to investigate the Republican theft of the 2000 election and I questioned the Bush Administration explanation of September 11 and asked for an independent investigation.
- I defied the Democratic Leadership that instructed Democrats to stay away from a Congressional Panel created to investigate the government's response to Hurricanes Katrina and Rita. Not only did I participate, I held a town hall meeting in New Orleans, received testimony from residents there, and invited residents to Washington, DC to tell their stories directly, without filter, to the Congressional Panel from which Democrats had been banned. I wrote important legislation based on what I learned.
- I filed Articles of Impeachment against George W. Bush and was the only Democratic Member of Congress to lose reelection in 2006.

The significance of that 2006 election loss was this: The very first bill to fund the war came up for a House vote and passed with exactly the number of votes required. Had I been there to cast my no vote, the bill would have failed. Today, we would be talking about our peace dividend. Like free tuition through the Ph.D. for students, or free health care for all in need.

One vote does make a difference.

After I left Congress in 2007, I declared my independence from the national leaders who made this country, with my tax dollars, complicit in war crimes, torture, crimes against humanity, and crimes against the peace. I declared my independence from every bomb dropped, every threat leveled, every civil liberties rollback, every child killed, every veteran maimed, every man tortured as a part of the U.S. war machine. So, I switched from just talking about it to doing even more about it.

There are many people in this country who are courageous resisters. And they wear the scars of sacrifice to prove it. But we need help if disaster is to be averted. While in the Congress, I tried to mainstream Black issues, but shockingly, Blacks who try to mainstream Black issues are being replaced by Blacks who won't. And the Black community is tolerating this.

I do believe that racism in the global social structure is a curable disease—if we take the action necessary to eradicate the disease. I believe that purposeful participation in policy-making can narrow existing gaps and make life easier for those living in life's shadows today. I do believe that we can slow the slide to chaos in store for us all if we choose to resist in this important moment.

VERNELLIA RANDALL has been Professor of Law at Dayton University Law School since 1990.She writes extensively on and speaks internationally about race, women, and health care. She is the recipient of the Ohio Commission on Minority Health Chairman's Award. Professor Randall provided public health nursing services and served as an administrator for a statewide health program in Alaska. Involved in public health work for more than 15 years, Professor Randall focused on eliminating disparities in health care for minorities and the poor. Professor Randall has also served as a grant reviewer for the National Institute of Health. She has been recognized in Who's Who in the World since 1995 and Who's Who in the United States since 1998. Professor Randall is the editor and webmaster for four academic websites on race, health care, gender, and academic support. She is the author of "Dying While Black". More importantly, she is the proud mother of her adult sons, Tshaka and Issa and the Nah-Nah of Ajani and Makai.

DYING
WHILE BLACK

VERNELLIA RANDALL

There has been something that has been weighing on my heart, and I want to say it briefly. I teach Racism and the Law and I cover every racism group, so any group with color. This year, after teaching it for over 24 years, for the first time something clicked in my mind and I am so distressed about it that: a) I did not notice it sooner; and b) that it is so far along. The idea of slavery did not happen overnight. Black people were not born into slavery, the slave system developed one wall at a time until, one day, the system was full blown. If you go back far enough, you can see where there were no black slaves. We don't get that talk, but there was a point in our history when there were no black slaves. There were black people in the United States and no black slaves! And then they developed the law until boom, suddenly we have alegal system called slavery. The same thing happened with Jim Crow. Coming out of slavery there was no Jim Crow, there was no segregation, there was no legal apartheid. It happened one law at a time. Wake up one day, what do you have? A whole system of discrimination entrenched in the law.

We now have another system already in place. It has two parts now, legally. The first part is the mass incarceration that makes people slaves for life once they become a felon under the law. The second part is the "kill at will" laws—I refuse to call them "stand your ground" laws. What that brings about is legal lynching, terrorizing black people as violence that can be legally perpetrated on black people. You have police that can perpetrate violence, and now you have the everyday citizens that can perpetrate violence. We have reinstituted a color blind legal apartheid. And it's in place. And we have to do something about it. This is an important issue for me and I wanted to bring it up.

My area of research is on black health and systematic changes that need to be made in order to improve black health. And I call it Dying While Black.

Every year 80,000 to 100,000 black people die that would not die if we had the same death rate as whites. What does that mean? It means that a jumbo jet full of nothing but black people would have to crash every day for a year to be able to get to 80,000 to 100,000 excess deaths. I thought about that and I tried to put it into context. One of the reasons I started trying to put it into context is that I stumbled upon a CIA quote that said that the quality of life of a people can be judged by their life expectancy. Wow, I said. This is official US policy. *If you want to know the quality of the life of a country look at the life expectancy.* So I thought: what if we compared African Americans as if they were a country. How do we stand? What is our quality of life?

I took this from the 2011 CIA World Factbook page, "Life expectancy at birth is ...a measure of overall quality of life in a country..." So I thought, that is a good way for us to think about where we are as African Americans. Before I move on, I need to make one thing clear: when I talk about African Americans, I talk about African Americans because I am African American. I am not building a hierarchy of pain. I am not suggesting that black people have worse health or are in more pain. We all have our pain and it hurts.

Look at this. Black American females. Our life quality in the US, based on the CIA Fact Book, is worse that of Cuba, Barbados, Bosnia, and the Bahamas. The Males: Chile, Barbados, Bahamas, and Jamaica. I picked out all these poor black countries to show that they have a better quality of life that black people in America, according to the CIA.

Life Expectancy – Males*

Rank	State	Years
1	San Marino	80
2	Japan	79
9	Canada	78
30	Cuba	76
	White American Males	**76**
35	Chile	75
44	Barbados	72
57	Bahamas	71
75	Jamaica	69
	Black American Males	**69**

Life Expectancy – Females*

1	Japan	86
4	Switzerland	84
9	Canada	83
29	United Kingdom	81
	White American Female	**81**
33	Cuba	80
39	Barbados	79
46	Bosnia and Herzegovina	78
55	Bahamas	77
	Black American Female	**77**

One of the things that we all know, but it helps to know it, is that it is not about class alone. When you compare within class you have the same discrepancies: poor whites live longer than poor blacks, middles class whites live longer than middle class blacks. So you think that being middle class is going to save you, but no.

My theory is that you have slavery, legal apartheid, and racism that have all contributed to the historical oppression and deprivation that has resulted in embedded racial inequalities in every area of black life. And while we can argue about individual behavior, I can also tell you that my change in my behavior is not going to do much of anything about the overall health status of black people, because it is due to all these inequalities. And most of these are due to chronic stress. When you think about it, what is the difference between middle class white people and middle class black people? It ain't money. Maybe a little about money, but not enough to make a difference. And it is also not about the choices: we go to the gym, we are exercising and doing all this stuff. But we have the chronic stress of racism and discrimination in our daily lives and that is the difference.

So how does this all relate to the law? I've taught criminal law, I've taught tort law, and I've taught discrimination law, and in two, in the law we try to recognize a continuum of legal behavior that we hold responsible. So, yes, if you intentionally do something we are going to hold you responsible. But we also hold people that did not intend their actions responsible as well. We say: you should have known. When you spilled that water on the floor and left it there, you should have known that someone was going to walk and slip and fall. You may have not intended it, but you should have known: that's negligence. And the strict liability is that we do not care if you should have known or if you intended it— if you do the act, you are responsible, period. Guess what? Two areas of law recognize the whole continuum in some way. Intentional, negligence, strict liability. Guess which area doesn't. Discrimination. The

*2008 World Health Organization and 2008 Health, United States

result is that there are all kinds of discrimination that is legal in the US. All kinds of discrimination, reckless discrimination, negligent discrimination, and strict liability discrimination is legal in the United States because the law does not recognize it.

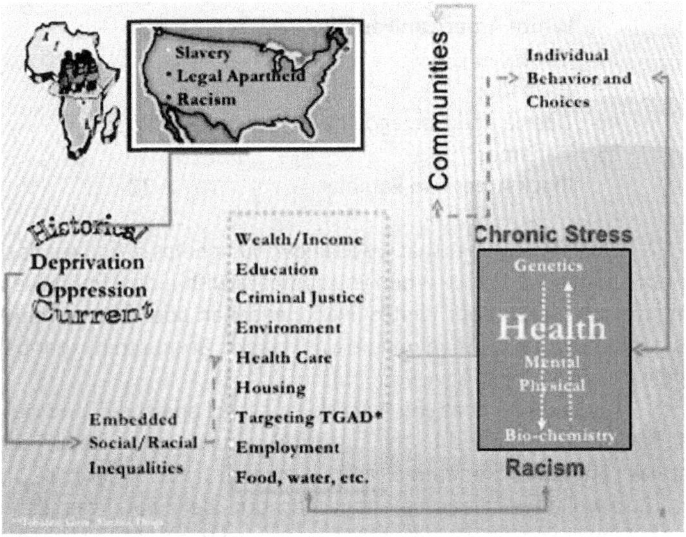

Inadequacy of Legal Efforts to Eliminate Racial Discrimination

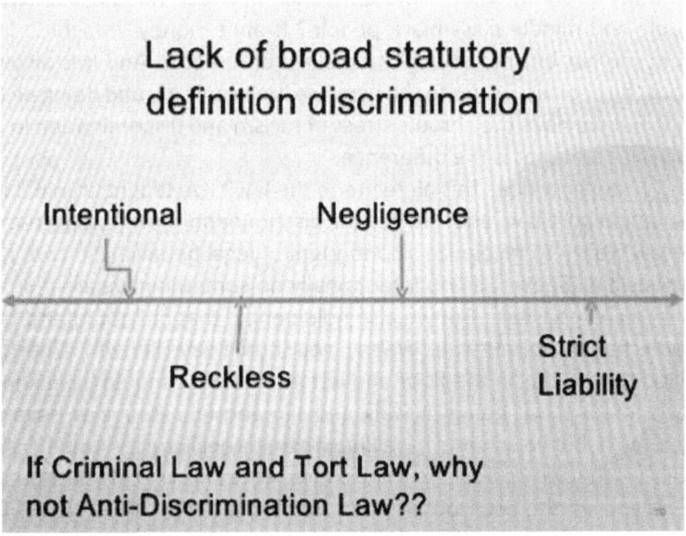

I want to talk about why this is a violation of the International Convention of the Elimination of All Forms of Racial Discrimination,[1] which is a treaty that the US has signed. However, there is a caveat—the United States is not dumb, if they sign on to a treaty they are not going to sign on in way that give you any rights. Nevertheless, it might be able to embarrass them.

The treaty says that you have to eliminate all forms of discrimination and that discrimination includes purpose and effect.

Article 2(1)(A) says:

> Each State Party undertakes to engage in no act or practice of racial discrimination against persons, groups of persons, groups of persons or institutions and to ensure that all public authorities and public institutions, national and local, shall act in conformity with this obligation.

Article 2(1)(c)says:

> Each State Party shall *take effective measures* to review governmental, national and local policies, and to *amend, rescind or nullify any laws and regulations which have the effect of creating or perpetuating racial discrimination* wherever it exists.

In the United States we only really recognize purposeful discrimination and we have done away with the ability to sue for effect discrimination. Most people don't realize that if you could collect the statistics to show that an organization was discriminating against black people, all you could do is complain, you cannot go into court on it. Article 2(1)(d) requires the United States to take action to prohibit discrimination. It states:

> Each State Party *shall prohibit and bring to an end,* by all appropriate means, including legislation as required by circumstances, racial discrimination by any persons, group or organization.

It cannot just say in relation to a state, "what can I do, the state won't allow me to do anything". It is a national government, it signed on to the treaty, it is supposed to do something about the states.

Article 5 says:

States Parties undertake to prohibit and to eliminate racial discrimination in all its forms and *to guarantee the right* of everyone, without distinction as to race, color, or national or ethnic origin, to equality before the law, notably *in the enjoyment of the following rights.*

These include:

- Equal treatment before the tribunals
- Security of person and protection against violence or bodily harm
- Political rights
- Civil rights
- Economic, social and cultural rights, including to health and housing
- Access to any place or service intended for use by the general public

It goes on to say that there can be no discrimination in relation to a wide range of civil rights. Article 5(e) says you have economic, social and cultural rights, in particular:

- The rights to work,
- To free choice of employment,
- To just and favorable conditions of work,
- To protection against unemployment
- To equal pay for equal work
- To just and favorable remuneration;
- To form and join trade unions;
- To housing
- The right to education and training;
- Equal participation in cultural activities;
- Access to any place or service intended for use by the general public, such as transport hotels, restaurants, cafes, theatres and parks

It does not guarantee the right, which would be wonderful if they said that you have all these economic and sociopolitical rights, it does not give you the rights, but it does say, is that there cannot be discrimination in providing the rights. So my thesis and other studies show that there is a large disparity that is occurring in all forms of economic rights.

What do we need the United States to do, and get it to do by putting pressure on it? I think that we have to talk about actions, even next steps.

We need a 21st century anti-discrimination law. Note that I did not call it a civil rights law. We are not talking about civil rights law. We are talking about eliminating all forms of discrimination, we should call it that.

An Effective 21st Anti-Discrimination Law would:

- Recognize multiple forms of discrimination (Intentional, reckless, negligent, strict liability)
- Allow both individual and organizational right of action
- Require deep data collection and reporting
- Make all providers and institutions responsible
- Pay Prevailing Plaintiff's Attorney Fees
- Allow Punitive Damages and collect into a fund to provide for health care services and antidiscrimination enforcement.

We need to recognize multiple forms of discrimination. Now that is going to be difficult because the people that make law, makes laws for other communities that protect their own community. So they are never going to make a law that really impinges upon their own community; they are always looking to see how is this going to affect their own community. So coming up with this will be revolutionary. *Getting a law that recognizes reckless discrimination will really revolutionize discrimination in our society.*

We need organizational rights. The only way you can get into court now is if you get hit on the head and sue. Most discrimination is behind the scenes and you do not even know when you have been discriminated against. We should allow organizations to collect statistics and to go into court and sue. Attorney fees, put that in, and then you will get lawsuits.

Finally, punitive damages. We have to go after institutional systemic discrimination. The only way to get institutions and systems to change is to hit them hard where they hurt. And that means winning awards for punitive damages. So any time you hear people arguing about limiting punitive damages, what they are basically saying is: we do not want to change and we want to limit your ability to make us change.

ENDNOTES

1 <http://www2.ohchr.org/english/law/cerd.htm>

TYSON KING-MEADOWS, Ph.D. is Associate Professor of Political Science at the University of Maryland Baltimore County. There he also holds affiliations with the Department of Public Policy, the Department of Africana Studies, and the Honors College. His general field of expertise is American politics, and his specializations include black political engagement, racial representation, and identity group politics. He is author of *When the Letter Betrays the Spirit: Voting Rights Enforcement and African American Participation from Lyndon Johnson to Barack Obama* (Lexington Books/Rowman and Littlefield, 2011) and co-author of *Devolution and Black State Legislators: Challenges and Choices in the Twenty-First Century* (State University of New York Press, 2006). Prof. King-Meadows is president of the National Conference of Black Political Scientists (NCOBPS).

FROM HALLOWED VICTORIES TO HOLLOW VICTORIES

POST CIVIL RIGHTS AND THE POST-RACIAL IMAGINATION

TYSON KING-MEADOWS

We are going to talk about these embedded social inequalities and tie it back to this thing called identity politics. So this a moment of intense questioning. It's a moment about questioning the role of the U.S. government, the demographic composition of the leaders of the American government, and whether there really is persistent racial injustice. In short, America must confront a host of questions about the relevance of a painful past to these sorts of lawsuits that discuss these circumstances. So it is really about what America believes America is.

Let me start with saying this: I am using two different constructs. First, the known reality versus the imagined reality, what I call the post-racial imagination. And hallowed victories versus hollowed victories. Simply put, no reality is what we as miners' canaries understand this experience, as race and gendered individuals living in a society with toxic gases racism, sexism, homophobia, classism, and over the top incivility. Not only have we as miners' canaries signaled time and time again that these gases are toxic to the health of the American democracy, we've called into question their addictive nature. So just as individuals communicate even when they shouldn't, we know that people are engaging in sexism and racism because they are addicted to the power that is inherent in it. Because some continue to take deep breaths, we wonder whether the fumes of racial and gender-based patriarchy have warped the minds of reasonable people. What else can explain the persistent hyperbolic racialized rhetoric used to describe the current president and the not so thinly veiled attacks against the president's supporters and anyone who dissents?

Many of you may recall that in September 2010, there was a *Village Voice* article that had a cartoonish display of Rush Limbaugh, Glen Beck, Laura Schlessinger, and Sarah Palin and the title was very simple: "White America Has Lost Its Mind: The white brain beset with worries finally goes haywire in this spectacular fashion". It wasn't just that 42% of Americans believed that Obama is Muslim. It's not that a quarter of Americans believe that Obama was probably born in another country. It's that white America has lost its sole possession of the leadership of the executive branch. And that brings what the author, Thrasher, called dementia. As you know dementia is a chronic disorder caused by brain disease or injury marked by memory disorders and other cognitive impairments. And that's the key, cognitive impairments. So expanding upon Thrasher's insight, I called the problem, the post-racial imagination. It's not just about white baby boomers and young Americans, it is also about how individuals conceptualize their identity and conceptualize the victories of the civil rights movement. The post-racial imagination does not see racism, sexism, and homophobia as present day toxins. Rather the post-racial imagination sees these things as fossils of the past that were detoxified by the hallowed victories of the civil rights movement. It's not just that the post-racial imagination says that racism does not exist, it plays on the very syntax of the term "civil rights movement". It pushes it to its logical and legal conclusion. It says the civil rights movement stopped because we won. The movement stopped because the laws were changed. The movement stopped because Bull Connor and George Wallace lost. The movement was relevant, but is no longer relevant. Civil rights are hallowed victories and anything that might seem like intentional discrimination are now individual choices that people make. So let me repeat, the post-racial imagination reveres these victories as evidence of a new day and says that the new day is here. So if the new day is here, then complaints about systemic racial injustice are hyperbolic.

That is why scholars are talking about how freedom is not enough. You actually need the effective enforcement of civil rights law. And we can argue about whether current or former presidents have effectively enforced civil rights law, but let's step aside from that. Though I do want to tell you about this one moment in 2008. Abigail Thurnstrom, who is a political scientist like myself, and is an early critic of affirmative action and redistricting, is also the vice chair of the U.S. Commission of

Civil Rights. So right after the race speech that Obama gave, she wrote in *The National Review* that she liked Obama's speech because of its, "subtlety, seriousness, and patriotism." But then she asked: what other contemporary prominent black politician could or would have given such a speech? From there, she goes on to indict the civil rights movement by saying, "Reverend Wright, as Obama says, is the product of a certain era thankfully gone as are Jesse Jackson, John Lewis, and most civil rights icons he could have added. Do I wish Senator Obama had walked away from Trinity Church? Sure. I suspect the reasons he did not do so are psychologically complex. In any case, afrocentric "Hate America" views are clearly not the views of Obama himself who lives in the country he says is the only country on Earth where his story is even possible."

So here I am not trying to reanimate a dead horse, but what she is trying to do is to talk about the impact, the psychological complexion, of the notion that African Americans have rights that they need to put forward. And to claim those as a hate-America view is a way of saying that the African American identify is somehow juxtaposed to the American identity.

And so these ideas about rights are a way of saying that you have narrow claims about justice. That these narrow claims have no place in the legal space. And so right before the 2008 democratic convention there was an article in the *New York Times Magazine* called "Is Obama the end of black politics?" It wasn't about "Is Obama the end of black office-seeking", but "Is Obama the end of black politicians asking for a redress of their grievances? Is Obama the end of this discussion on civil rights?" Because if Obama wins, then all of a sudden civil rights are no longer necessary.

The Obama victory, for some, allows critics to say: look there are no longer myopic party politics. For some, an Obama victory means that you can never evoke "no two seats" to represent the contours of contemporary exclusion. And if Obama wins you can no longer stand up and talk about the *Voting Rights Act* as a prophylactic against white racial voting and white discrimination. Because clearly Obama won, so we might not need the *Voting Rights Act* any more. And so the attack on the *Voting Rights Act* is a way of saying you don't need this policy, this law, because, look, you have achieved. And that is a dangerous space for people to be in intellectually, cognitively. It's dangerous to buy into the post-racial imagination. Because the post-racial imagination suggests that there unicorns and dragons just as well as suggests that there is no longer racism. If you can believe that there is no longer racism, then I can convince you that there are unicorns and dragons.

The problem with the post-racial imagination is that we never get beyond the fantasy. We never want to talk about the statistics because there are statistics and there are lies, and there are lies that use statistics. So whenever someone talks about using a statistic as a way of redressing grievances, individuals talk about choice. For example, when individuals sue Louisville and Seattle over the voluntary school desegregation policies, the answer is that black families could simply move to other cities, to other neighborhoods. Well if the research coming out of MIT and the University of Chicago are correct, parents named Lakisha and Jamal are less likely to get the jobs that allow them to have economic mobility. So let's think about this sequentially. If you don't get a good job, then you are probably going to get a subprime loan. If you get a subprime loan and do not have affordable housing, you might be trapped in a particular area. And in that area, people live a particular way. So I'm not just talking about sociology when work disappears. I'm talking about the systematic and integrated nature of oppression. When parents try to get out of an old neighborhood and get into a new neighborhood, the critique the Supreme Court pushed back is that there is no compelling state interest. Think about it linguistically: there is no compelling state interest. You might have a state interest, but it might not be compelling. You might have a compelling interest but it does not rise to the level of a state action. But those are the hallowed victories of the civil rights movement.

So you can take *Brown* and hollow it out by saying: look, if you really want to have better schools, just be in better neighborhoods and ignore the opportunity structure that is presented by new redliners. And so you have the Supreme Court decision in 2007 that virtually says that we are not going to get into this because these are individual choices. If you raise it to "individual choices", the post-racial imagination allows you to just sit and see unicorns because I cannot see systematic discrimination. And in fact it looks like you have chosen to be in the position that you are in.

The second thing I will talk about are these new voter ID laws. These new voter ID laws say to you that if you want to vote, you need to go and get an ID from a government sponsored entity. But if, at the same time, you defund the places where you can get a license, if you move them somewhere else, or you eliminate them, that's problematic. Or at the same time you say that you will only accept particular forms of identification to prove who you are, like a birth certificate. So what happens if we were to ask your great grandmother if she still had her birth certificate? There are some places in the South where there are no official birth certificates. So when the NAACP's report at the end of December in 2011 is calling questions and saying to the UN that, hey, there are some questions you need to ask, it's not because these things happen by chance. They happen because they are systematically put into place as if it were coincidental. Because I can construct something to make you think that it is coincidental when it actually is not coincidental.

But the post-racial imagination wants you to think that the hallowed victories are sacred. That's not so when you can hollow them out like a donut. But there are not a lot that are going to break the law, but you can bend the law. So after *Brown* we see that there are some places in America where people are more segregated in their educational environment then they were before *Brown*. And it's connected to these housing structures which are connected to labor market participation, which are connected to the bank industry.

So let me conclude here. If the Supreme Court has ruled that we get rid of the all-white primary, which we did, and we got rid of the poll taxes in state elections through a Supreme Court ruling. We got rid of it in federal elections through the constitutional amendment. We got rid of voter disenfranchisement through literacy tests and character exams. However those hallowed victories of the civil rights movement are being hollowed out piece by piece. What was a victory to make democracy whole is being hollowed out like a doughnut. We can talk about these victories as they were in the past, but we should talk about them and what they mean now, today. The question for today is: does America have enough political will to make these victories whole again in the age of Obama and to reject the belief that there are unicorns and there is something called the post-racial imagination.

PANEL TWO

INTERNAL SELF-DETERMINATION FOR HISTORICALLY OPPRESSED PEOPLES

- What is internal self-determination?
- Are there any institutional or constitutional options other than assimilation or secession?
- What is the difference between affirmative action and internal self-determination?
- What are some possible forms of internal self-determination exercised by other internal nations elsewhere, or even here in the United States
- What can we learn from the successful practices of other states for ensuring minority cultural protection and equal-status development?
- Do the peoples exercising internal self-determination have to be territorially based or are there non-territorial options?

Left to right: Speakers Prof. Daniel Turp, Dr. Ava Muhammad, Prof. Carla D. Pratt and moderator Mary A. Mitchell.

DANIEL TURP studied law at the Université de Montréal and the University of Ottawa, and received his legal license in Sherbrooke. He gained a Master's degree at the Université de Montréal and Doctorate (summa cum laude) from Pantheon-Assas Paris II University. He is a professor at the Faculty of Law of the Université de Montréal since 1982. He lectures in the area of Public International Law, International and Constitutional Human Rights Law and Advanced Constitutional Law. Professor Turp served as member of the House of Commons of Canada for Beauharnois-Salaberry from 1997 to 2000 and was the Bloc Québécois' critic for Foreign and Intergovernmental Affairs. Professor Turp was also member of Québec's National Assembly from 2003 to 2008 and the spokeperson of the Parti Québécois on International Relations, Intergovernmental Affairs, Culture and Justice He has published extensively in the areas of international and constitutional law as well on Québec and Canada's political future. His latest legal and political essays have been published under the titles *The Right to Choose: Essays on Québec's Right to Self-Determination* and *The Muzzled Nation: Plan B or Ottawa's Offensive against Québec.*

EXTERNAL SELF-DETERMINATION AND INTERNAL SELF-DETERMINATION IN QUEBEC, CANADA

DANIEL TURP

I was invited to talk about self-determination in the Quebec context. Although there are parallels to be made between the black communities in the United States and may be more parallels when in the previous conferences[1] we were discussing not only Quebec, but the Islets, and Scotland, and what's happening in many parts of the world where there are peoples making claims for self-determination, whether internal or external, I think that self-determination is all about freedom. It's all about peoples as collectivities claiming more freedom, more say in everyday life. I would like to talk to you about what has happened in Quebec in the past decades, but also about what is happening now because self-determination is a continuing process. A great French philosopheronce said that a nation is a plebiscite of every day— a process where every day you decide who you are, what you are, and what you'd like to be or become. Quebec in that respect has been struggling for self-determination and continues to do on a day to day basis.

Quebec is one of the 10 providences of Canada. There are also 3 territories in Canada. It is a federal system like the US but is seen as a more centralized system, because provinces have a great amount of power in many areas. It's a country of 33 million inhabitants, Quebec has now in this Fall has reached 8 million people, 23% of Canada's population as a whole. Though that portion is going down significantly. At one point it was 35%, but the population of the western providences of Canada, including BC, is increasing more than that of Quebec, so the number of Quebecers in proportion is less than it was in the past decade.

Within Quebec, of that 8 million people, there is about 80%, a little bit more than 80%, that are French-speaking or of French origin. There is a national minority of English-speaking Quebecers that composes about 8% of the Quebec population now. There are immigrants of all sorts. In the early '50s-'60s, there were Italian and Greek immigrants, now more are coming from French-speaking Arab countries, and they are about 10% of the population now, and increasing. And there are 11 aboriginal nations in Quebec. There are 10 Indian nations, and 1 "inuit" nation, who comprise somewhat more than 1% of the population, approximately 100,000 inhabitants. So that is the graphic outlook of Quebec nowadays.

Originally, Quebec was New France, but there was a conquest in 1759, so New France became Canada. But Canada then was comprised of both Quebec, and Ontario, and part of the United States. Afterwards, Canada became upper and lower Canada, and then it became a Confederation in 1867 where Quebec was one of four providences then. Canada was not a country, Canada only became a country for our Supreme Court of Canada between 1949 and 1982. It relinquished progressively its links with the United Kingdom and the British Empire. But even then it took another three decades before Canada became completely independent because until 1982 Canada could not even amend its own constitution, it could only be amended in Britain by the British Parliament.

Then in 1982 there was the patriation of the Canadian constitution—a total partriation from the UK, which made Canada a totally independent country. That was not long ago, only some 30 years ago. The 1982 patriation of the Canadian Constitution triggered a lot of difficulties for Quebec, because it was done unilaterally—without Quebec's consent. And we, the French Quebeckers (Québécois) did not celebrate it. The 1982 constitution entered into force on April 17th, 1982 and the Queen came to Ottawa. Mr. Trudeau, the Canadian Prime Minister, and others were very proud of the patriation of the constitution, but all of that was done without Quebec's consent. Even though Quebec did not agree with what was in this new constitution, and had been isolated by the other 9 provinces, the federal government still went ahead and asked the United Kingdom to adopt this constitution and it did. Since 1982, Quebec has never signed on to that constitution and is not part of that constitution. It has been imposed on Quebec because the Supreme Court has said that Canada can go ahead and adopt the constitution without Quebec's consent and that it still applies to Quebec.

There has been, throughout the history of Quebec, the idea that it should continue to exist. At one point Canada was Quebec, Canada was French-speaking Canadians and the others were not Canadian, they were English. And then they became English Canadians and we became French Canadians. And then in early '60s the French Canadians came to identify themselves more and more as Quebecers, and also at that point, in 1967, the idea took hold that Quebec formed a nation in itself, the Quebec nation.

Quebec has always been in survival mode and always wanted to survive and exist. And it tried. And it made a lot of children. My grandmother had a lot of children. Now we do not have many children, we have a very low birth rate, but Quebec survived. During all those years and decades and centuries, there was always the idea that we were a nation and wanted to continue. We had an identity; we wanted to preserve that identity. The idea that the Québécois were to be assimilated was not acceptable. We t wanted to preserve our language, our culture, and in those days there was also the issue of preserving the Catholic faith, because the French in Quebec were Catholic. So we were intent on preserving that kind of identity: native language, culture, religion. And in the '60s what we called the Quiet Revolution took place. At one point, many Quebecers said: "It is really hard to survive in Canada, it is really hard to be ourselves and have our own identity. Let's think about may be becoming a country. Maybe becoming a country on our own."

Québec's Right of Self-Determination

Since then there has been a big debate where self-determination—the notion of self-determination—has played a key role. In the '60s, the right of self-determination was being advocated and used by colonial peoples in Africa and in the Pacific. The Québécois said: "We also are an oppressed people in a sense. Our language is not respected and we do not have our own institutions, or if we do, we cannot use them like we want to develop ourselves, let's become a country."

And that's when the leaders of political parties started to invoke the right of self-determination under international law. They would quote the Charter of the United Nations, and the 1966 Covenants on human rights where common article one in both Covenants says: "All peoples have the right of self-determination. By virtue of that right they freely determine their political status and freely pursue their economic, social and cultural development." In Quebec, the political life organized itself around this idea: that Quebec had the right to self-determination and could decide for itself what should be its political status. There were people advocating full independence from Canada, and still do. Some people were advocating changing the federal system, making

Quebec more autonomous within Canada and trying then to change the constitution and to gain more powers over the economy and to become recognized as a distinct society or nation within the Canadian framework.

In the '60s, political parties in Quebec were advocating for one or the other of the options, and at one point—it was a shock for many people, may be even in the US—the political party led by a very charismatic leader, Rene Levesque, won the election in Quebec in 1976. It was very surprising; people never thought it would happen. But Quebecers decided that they would give this new party, a social democratic party which had also an interesting program on social issues and the environment, a chance, and it was elected. It was elected on the commitment that it would hold a referendum that would be on the idea of becoming independent, of having some kind of special relationship with Canada that would then be another different country, but with whom we would maintain a special relationship because it was our neighbor and we had great economic ties of great importance that shouldn't be severed. And the idea of that political party, the Parti Québécois, was to have a sovereign Quebec and a relationship with the rest of Canada which would be analogous to what is happening in Europe and what is happening with the European community, now the European Union where countries were in a very close economic relationship, but remained different sovereign countries when it came to all the other issues: culture language, religion, social issues.

The Parti Québécois organized the first referendum in 1980 and it was an interesting democratic exercise. We adopted a Referendum Act that created two umbrella committees and strict rules on how much money could be spent by each of the two committees to promote the yes and no sides. It ended up with a defeat of the yes side. It was 40% for sovereignty association and 60% in favor of against sovereignty association.

In the campaign, what still upsets a lot of people in Quebec, is that in 1980 during that time Mr. Trudeau (who was from Quebec) was the prime minister of Canada, he promised the Québécois solemnly that if they voted "no" there would be changes to Canadian constitution that would allow Quebecers to be freer, and to have more autonomy. But what Mr. Trudeau then did two years later was to adopt a constitution without at all dealing with the fundamental issues that were important to Quebec. He put in a Charter of Human Rights and Freedoms in the constitution from London, but he made a deal with Premiers of the 9 other provinces and went on to patriate the constitution without Quebec's consent.

Now the constitution of 1982 even repealed parts of Quebec language laws without its consent and that still has consequences today because the Supreme Court sometimes makes decisions that are very inconsistent with Quebec's view on what should be its own language policy. So in 1982 the patriation of the Canadian constitution left people in Quebec very upset, and then there were attempts later on to repair the injustice of the constitutional negotiations led by Mr. Malroney, the Conservative Party leader who became the next prime minster in Ottawa. He tried to negotiate a new constitutional agreement to bring back Quebec into the Canadian family constitutionally. There was the Meech Lake Accord, which was not adopted. And a few years later there was the Charlottetown Accord. There was a referendum both in Quebec and the rest of Canada. This referendum to change the constitution was defeated again because in Quebec people said that this Agreement was not giving enough autonomy to Quebec while the rest of Canada in 1992 said it gave too much autonomy to Quebec, and for very different reasons. There was a vote and 56% were against the Charlottetown Accord in Quebec while 54% in the rest of Canada voted against it. The Parti Québécois was reelected in 1994 on the promise to hold another referendum on independence. One year after reelection it held the referendum, and in the meantime, a new party was created in Ottawa, the Bloc Québécois. Together these political parties and other movements promoted the idea of sovereignty with the same kind of idea—that even though we become sovereign, there should still be a special partnership with Canada that is economic, maybe also political, some kind of common citizenship between Canada and Quebec. And that referendum, the second one on the issue of independence, was held on Oct 30th, 1995. The result was a very narrow margin of 49.42% "Yes" to 50.58% "No". That was a bit upsetting for some of us, but that's democracy.

We were very upset whent we realized that a lot of people had cheated and that our laws had not been respected, because there was so much money spent illegally on the vote, which did not respect our referendum laws. All kinds of things happened that were unacceptable, such as Canada's accelerating the granting of citizenship to some recent immigrants so they could vote no. But still, the referendum was lost.

There was talk about self-determination. People would say we have the right to decide our own future, there was nothing in the constitution that said that. That is the struggle—to gain that right for ourselves, even if it is not in the constitution itself, even if under international law it is not very obvious because maybe it only applies to colonial peoples, but the struggle—the idea that we were people, and that we had the right to decide our future— finally was accepted by other Canadians and the Canadian government. So it means a lot to struggle and persevere on your own for what you think is your right and your responsibility: to maintain your identity and to fight for your identity.

Québec's Right to International and Internal Self-Determination and the Supreme Court of Canada

But that was difficult because when we almost won in 1995, people said, ok let's use the law now. Let's give the Supreme Court of Canada the chance to say that Quebecers have the right to separate from Canada. There were three questions put to the Supreme Court in 1998, asking the court if Quebec had the right to self-determination under international law that would allow it to unilaterally secede? Is there a right to secede under Canadian constitutional law? And another other dealing with the conflict between international law and constitutional law. That was really interesting. The government of Quebec boycotted that case because it said that this was political and was not legal, but the court decided to decide on the issue. Surprisingly it gave an advisory opinion that refused to bluntly answer the questions. It suggested that international law did not allow Quebec to secede unilaterally from Canada because Quebec was not a colonial people under the definition of the UN and it was not an oppressed people.

But on the question relating to internal self-determination, the Supreme Court said under the principles of democracy and federalism, if there is a clear question for Quebecers and a clear majority, Quebec has a right to secede under Canadian constitutional law. And there is even an obligation on the other partners of the federation to negotiate Quebec secession. There are two issues: the question should be clear and there has to be a clear majority. It did not say what kind of questions would be deemed to be clear and what was a majority. Then the federal parliament adopted the Clarity Act that suggested that the questions should never deal with the issue of sovereignty with partnership (sovereignty-association), because that would not be clear. The question would need to be: do you want to be independent and that is all. And on the clarity of what constitutes a majority, the Clarity Act is unclear.

So we have relied a lot on external self-determination, but now we can rely on internal self-determination under the Canadian constitution. Now the Supreme Court has suggested that we do have internal self-determination. So what has happened, since the beginning of the present century, is that there has been little movement on this issue of independence or self-determination, because in 2003 the Parti Québécois was defeated by the Liberal Party of Canada led by a federalist who does not want Quebec to secede, but he also does not want more autonomy for Quebec. He always says that the fruit is not ripe and we should not try and negotiate more because Canadians are not willing to give more autonomy to Quebec. So he has been very careful not to open Pandora's Box. Because if we try again to negotiate, it won't work and eventually another referendum will be organized because eventually Quebecers will be upset that no agreement has been reached on constutional autonomy and independence will become an issue once again.

But when you have a motion that is only a motion, that is not in the constitution, and that does not mean much except symbolically, people are not really satisfied.

Since the 1995 referendum, the successive Canadian governments have decided not to deal with the issue of Québec self-determination. This might end soon because elections have to be called in the next year. If the Parti Québécois is elected, the future is about self-determination and hopefully Quebecers will continue to democratically be able to decide what they want to become and will, I hope, decide to emerge as a free, democratic and independent nation.

[NOTE: Since the delivery of this paper, the Parti Québécois has been returned to power in Quebec.]

ENDNOTES

1 IHRAAM Conferences on the right to self-determination held in Geneva in 2000 and 2004. See Y.N. Kly and D. Kly, eds., *In Pursuit of the Right to Self-Determination: Collected Papers &Proceedings of the First International Conference on the Right to Self-determination & the United Nations, Geneva 2000*, Clarity Press, Inc., 2001 and Y.N. Kly & D. Kly, eds., *In Pursuit of an International Civil Tribunal on the Right to Self-determination: Collected Papers 7 Proceedings of the Second International Conference on the Right to Self-determination, the United Nations, and International Civil Society, Geneva 2004*, Clarity Press, Inc., 2005.

DR. AVA MUHAMMAD is the National Spokesperson for Minister Louis Farrakhan. She received her Bachelor of Arts in history from Central State University in Wilberforce, Ohio. In 1975, she received a Juris Doctor from Georgetown University Law School and was admitted to the New York Bar. Her earliest professional experience was in law enforcement, in the New York State Office of Child Support Enforcement and later served as an Assistant District Attorney in Queens, New York. In addition to being the author of several books and having been recognized by *Essence* as one of the 30 most influential Black women in America in 2000, Dr. Muhammad is a gifted lecturer and researcher which has placed her in great demand among colleges, universities, churches, conferences and radio programs. She has addressed the National Association of Black Social Workers, the NAACP Leadership Conference, the Million Woman March, the 40th Anniversary of the March on Washington in 2003. Dr. Muhammad is the first Muslim woman in modern history to occupy a position of authority over a mosque anywhere in the world. She served as the Nation of Islam's Southern Regional Minister from 1998 until 2000, after she was appointed a National Spokesperson for the Nation of Islam, a position she continues to hold this day.

SEEKING SOVEREIGNTY
THE NEED FOR AN IDENTIFIABLE PLACE

AVA MUHAMMAD

In order to have a really logical look or view of the viability of the descendants of African slaves in the United States of America being able to actually engage in self-determination in the absence of a defined territory within the continental United States, we have to look at the history of this country and look at the mindset of the Founding Fathers. And when we study U.S. history and the mindset of the Founding Fathers, keep in mind that the enslavement of our people preceded the existence of the United States. We were enslaved by Europeans invading West Africa, kidnapping people off the coast of West Africa, and bringing them against their will. It was not simply involuntary servitude or indentured servants. We're talking about torture. We're talking about rape, death, murder. And we're talking about a complete disconnect from the original homeland, language, culture, and religion of that people. And so by the time of the Declaration of Independence and United States Constitution, we had been here over 200 years in an enslaved subjugated condition.

It was never, ever, the intent of the Founding Fathers to include Black people in setting up this country for and by the people of the United States. We were not defined as people at the time of the U.S. Constitution and it has never been amended to correct that. And so we have to understand the original intent in bringing us to the United States was for labor to be performed. If you study the history of the presidency and U.S. Congress, in as early as the presidency of Thomas Jefferson, there were plans to take as many as slaves as could be let go and return them to Africa. There was no vision of black people coming off of plantations and moving around in society. That was a nightmare to the Founding Fathers. It was never contemplated.

Even as cirumstances changed and time passed, that did not happen. So although the 13th Amendment was passed, we have to understand as well that there were two 13th Amendments. The first 13th Amendment that was put before Congress just before the outbreak of the Civil War actually was written to ensure that slavery would exist in perpetuity. When the Civil War broke out, and with the succession of the southern states, Abraham Lincoln pretty much shoved through the 13th Amendment that abolished slavery because he did not want to act simply on executive order. The reality is that at the time the 13th Amendment was passed, most of the southern states were absent because they had seceded and formed another nation. To this day there has never been a consensus among the southern states that agreed to even the 13th Amendment. So you can then imagine their feeling towards the 14th Amendment establishing civil rights and 15th Amendment prohibiting racial voting restrictions.

And this is why there has been such a bloody struggle all these decades since the so-called granting of freedom via the Emancipation Proclamation, which was of course an executive order of the President and not an act of Congress. And so to counteract the reconstruction changes made during that period, in 1877 there was an agreement between the parties to return Black people to their state of servitude in order to have Benjamin Hayes elected president. Southern states were very angry over the presence of federal troops and over the election of Blacks to legislative positions and what they felt was the loss of control of their ex-slaves. And so there was an agreement on the federal government's part to withdraw from the South. That is when the domestic terrorism called Jim Crow entered into the picture.

I was in a setting recently where someone asked me, "Why is it that other people can come here from other countries with nothing, with immigrant status, and within a generation they are flourishing, and yet you are not and you don't seem to come together, and this sort of thing. And I said, "Well what you are not aware of is that we have done that. We did it in Tulsa, we did it in Rosewood, and we did it in more than 60 settlements around this country, coming right up out of 400 hundred years of servitude and being denied any right to read and write. And you imagine the back-breaking work on a southern plantation where no one talks to you at all and we cannot even fathom the developmental disability that a person suffers when they are not allowed to develop their own human potential."

I remember when we were visiting a plantation, or what had once been a plantation, in Charleston, South Carolina, a few years ago and the mansion they kept intact which is huge and beautiful. At that time, back in those days, it was a rural area, so you had to get where you were going either by walking or by horse and buggy, so 10 miles was quite a journey. But this mansion was left intact and they walk you through it and they show you what they now call the servant quarters. And what struck me as very profound, I saw there a letter by a young girl who had been taught to read and write by the wife of the plantation owner, and she was only 16 when she wrote this letter. She said in the letter to someone that the worst part of being a slave is not the work; the worst part is always having to think for someone else. "I wake up in the morning and my only thoughts are my mistress. Is she comfortable? Is she too hot? Is she too cold? What color does she want to wear? Is she happy with her dress? What does she want? I never give any thought to myself." And to me that expresses the quintessence of self-determination—freedom, justice and equality. The ability to be able to act out as a vicegerent of God, which all human beings are, to act freely in accordance with your own divine purpose.

Sovereignty, as I mentioned before, is absolute by definition. The US Supreme Court can say one thing and do another, it has a history of doing that. The US government has a history of saying one thing and doing another. And so the issue becomes whether or not there is any indication—historically, politically, economically, or legally— that we can exercise our right to self-determination in the absence of a defined territory. A lot of time people get nervous when you talk about separation because they think it means isolation or going off somewhere and having no contact with anyone else ever again. It does not mean that. It means sovereignty. It means a defined territory wherein you set your constitutional law. You set your legislation so that you are not always put in position that in order to gain anything you have to protest.

If you look at the current case of Trayvon Martin, there is something bizarre and really tragic that we have to have a national protest movement in order to obtain an arrest. In a case where you have a homicide and you have the shooter confessing to the homicide, and yet there is still this resistance to taking him into custody. And all of a sudden we're held to a standard normally required for a conviction, but we're required to meet that standard in order to even gain an arrest. And then, a period of time always elapses where we have to think about it. We have to investigate it. We have to look at it again. Why? Because the condition that exists today was not the intent of the Founding Fathers.

The key to a truly sovereign state is that the interests of the people of that state are guaranteed by the government. The people of that state have their interests put first; they are not subordinate to another people. And so the people decide the answer to the question: what will our educational system consist of? Well it will consist of a curriculum that facilitates our belief system, our ideology, our view and perception of ourselves. And at the end of the day everything is about perception. Our own perception is our reality. So, in order to have freedom, justice, and equality, you have to have some place identifiable where you know as a certainty that your perception of reality will be respected and that it will be given a way to work itself out without being crushed before it's even fully expressed.

And that is the basis of my presentation, because I think that this a very complex issue. But as we hear with Professor Turp's analysis of the situation of the people of Quebec, the question was not what the people there ultimately decided; what they were after most importantly was the freedom to make that decision. In our history here, we have never ever been able to be a part of the decision-making process. I see our beloved sister [referring to former Congresswoman Cynthia McKinney] who has stood up for us, a powerful voice in a powerful body, the U.S. Congress, who has been willing, as so many in our history have been willing to do, to sacrifice her financial stability, her career, and all those things inherent to the life that, as a human being when you achieve things, you are entitled to have. But simply because she tells the truth, she has to be heroic in order to be able to tell it. That is not self-determination when you have to lay down your life—not that we are not willing to do that, but our children should be able to walk to a store and get a bag of skittles and bottle of ice tea during the half-time of the NBA All Star Game and come back home alive. It is then that this issue of sovereignty becomes worthy of our review. Because other than that we'll be engaged in discussions about Sean Will and Oscar Grant and Amado Diallo and Trayvon Martin and the list goes on and on—and that's only those we know about. That's not those who we don't know about.

Someone said to me "We have gone back to Emmett Till." I said "No we haven't gone back to Emmett Till because in Emmett Till's time, they felt they had to have a trial, as phony as it was. They felt compelled to have a trial. Now there is no compulsion." We haven't been assured there will ever be litigation. You have a new law called Stand Your Ground, 'Shoot-At-Will', 'Shoot First', that extends law enforcement now to people that are not necessarily qualified to have a weapon, now you have the return of the vigilante, a euphemism for the Klu Klux Klan. So now my life depends on the perception of individual who may be a sociopath. That is not freedom, justice, and equality.

So we have to consider these things when we talk about the

viability of self-determination unless and until we can say, as the Mormons did in Utah—they didn't go and buy it, they didn't buy Utah—"We have a distinct faith, and everywhere we go to try to and practice this faith. We perceive ourselves as Christians. We don't perceive you as Christians. Well we do. So what we'll do since everywhere we go we get hung, we will keep going and going. We are going all the way out West to Utah and we will overpopulate the state of Utah." So now when you go to Utah, there are no gates, no law saying you cannot go, but don't go out there trying to go to Hooters because that is not their way of life.

The Amish want to live in a certain time in history that they find compatible with their mindset. "We aren't interested in all this modern technology. We do not like what it brings with it. So we are going to live out in rural areas the way we want to live." Does that mean they hate somebody? No. It simply means they are exercising their right to self-determination.

CARLA D. PRATT is Associate Dean for Academic Affairs and Professor of Law at Penn State University, Dickinson School of Law where she has taught courses in Constitutional Law, Race and American Law, and Criminal Law. Professor Pratt's scholarly interests examine the legal construction of racial identity and the role of race in the legal profession. Her research employs Critical Race Theory, to explore how law often unintentionally operates to perpetuate the subordination of racial minorities rather than achieve true equality. Her current research project examines tribal law's exclusion of blacks and posits that slaveholding Indian tribes have consistently viewed blacks as racially ineligible for tribal citizenship. Prior to entering academia, Professor Pratt practiced civil litigation in the NJ Attorney General's Office and the law firm of Drinker Biddle & Reath,, LLP in Philadelphia.

USING INTERNATIONAL HUMAN RIGHTS TO PROTECT INDIGENEITY

CARLA D. PRATT

Presently, two seemingly disparate areas of law—tribal law and international human rights law—are colliding. In the past several years, a number of Native American tribes have taken action to exclude people of African ancestry from tribal membership. This action contravenes treaties that guarantee certain African Americans citizenship in these tribes because of their historical relationship to the tribes.[1] Among these tribes is the Cherokee Nation of Oklahoma which, after losing a battle over tribal identity in its own courts, voted to exclude people known as the "freedman descendants" because the freedmen are the descendants of African slaves once held in bondage under Cherokee law.[2] Although some of these freedman descendants have Indian ancestry, many cannot prove it because tribal and federal records created during the late nineteenth and early twentieth centuries applied the rule of hypodescent, also known as the one-drop rule, to construct blacks with Indian ancestry as monoracial "negroes" thereby erasing all evidence of their Indian ancestry.

At the core of the freedman debate is the issue of what it means to be Indian and who gets to decide. Of course the U.S. Supreme Court has already addressed the issue of who gets to decide tribal membership. In the 1978 landmark case of *Santa Clara Pueblo v. Martinez*[3], the Supreme Court held that the doctrine of tribal sovereignty gives to tribes the power of self- determination and that inherent in this power of self-determination is the power to determine the tribe's own membership. Accordingly, under current federal law, unless Congress has exercised its plenary power over tribes in a way that abridges their tribal sovereignty, tribes may determine the criteria for citizenship even where the criteria used discriminates against a particular class of individuals in a way that would violate the Equal Protection Clause of the U.S. Constitution if done by a state.

In other words, it is perfectly lawful for a Native American tribe or nation to exclude individuals from the tribe on the basis of race because the Equal Protection mandate found in the Fourteenth Amendment to the U.S. Constitution applies to constrain the power of the states and the federal government, not Indian tribes.[4] Although each tribe gets to decide for itself what it means to be a tribal member and what is required for membership, the Courts have also held that tribes do not have immigration power because that power resides exclusively with the federal government.[5] As a result of this rule, coupled with tribal history that grouped people into tribes on the basis of race and ancestral relationships, most tribes define eligibility for tribal membership in terms that require some proof of Indian "blood" which is demonstrated by tracing ancestry. Some tribes require proof of Indian blood through a blood quantum requirement which means that an individual must prove that a certain percentage of her ancestors were tribal members and that she is therefore a certain percentage of Indian blood. Other tribes have dispensed with the blood quantum requirements and merely require that an individual demonstrate an ancestral relationship to a single ancestral tribal member, no matter how remote in kinship. Regardless of the methodology, federal law provides that each tribe decides who is eligible for tribal citizenship.[6] Because tribes have varying approaches to defining tribal membership, and because tribal membership has generally connoted that an individual is "Indian," the dispute around who can be a member of a tribe ultimately arises out of confusion about what it means to be Indian.

Defining Indianness is no simple task under either tribal law or federal Indian law. The U.S. Supreme Court in the case of *Morton v. Mancari*[7] held that Indian identity is a political identity and that hiring preferences granted to Native Americans are done on the basis of their political identity as members of a sovereign nation, not because of their racial identity. Accordingly, it is arguably tribal citizenship that makes one "Indian" since citizenship or membership in a tribe forms the political identity referenced by the Supreme Court. But when the individuals in question are black, this political conception of Indian identity gets subordinated to the historical notions of Indianness as a racial category.

The former slaveholding tribes' conception of Indianness

ignores international law and international conventions defining basic human rights. The freedmen and their descendants were made citizens of their respective tribes pursuant to their former slaveholding tribes' agreement with the federal government in the post- Civil War treaties of 1866. Hence, according to treaties agreed upon by the tribes and the federal U.S. government, the freedmen descendants are citizens of their respective tribes and therefore politically Indian, even if they do not have any Indian ancestry. Despite the treaties of 1866 mandating that the slaveholding Indian tribes adopt their freed slaves as full citizens of their respective tribes, the freedmen were never really integrated into the tribe as full citizens. Instead they faced opposition from tribal leaders who sought either to exclude them from tribal membership altogether, or at least separate and subordinate them from the "real Indians" – that being, those citizens with some measure of documented Native American ancestry, but with no known African ancestry.

Facially identifiable racial differences between persons classified as Native Americans and African Americans, along with the prevalence of the rule of hypodescent, commonly known as the one drop rule, applied to persons with any known African ancestry, made it difficult for tribal leaders to see the freedmen as Indian. Kinky hair and chocolate colored skin simply did not comport with the racialized conception of Native American identity that had been held by whites and indoctrinated into persons of Native American ancestry. As a result, individuals whose appearance revealed the presence of African ancestry were routinely denied tribal membership even when the individual was known to have Indian ancestors.[8]

Part of the rationale or justification for the tribes' willingness to engage in the practice of enslaving blacks was that they had been taught the race science by whites that held blacks as the lowest form of human beings lacking in intellect and morals and therefore appropriately subjugated to slavery status by the more enlightened and evolved races of Indians and whites. The slaveholding tribes' conception of themselves as a racial group was inevitable since the tribes existed within a nation whose founding document distinguished its inhabitants by race. Of course race is not a natural or biological or scientific category. It is a social construction – a way of classifying people that was created by social means. In separating people into three major racial groups in the U.S., the laws and society ascribed meaning to the physical features of individuals. Dark brown or black skin, kinky hair, wide noses and full lips were the physical identifiers of the "Negro" race; the race deemed so unenlightened and incapable of advancement that they were justifiably condemned to a life of slavery. Higher on the racial hierarchy was the "Indian" race with reddish skin, straight silky hair, narrow noses and thin lips. This group was deemed to be unenlightened, but capable of being cultivated into enlightened and productive participants in society. By the 19th century, slaveholding Indian tribes had incorporated the racialized understandings of whites and had fully adopted and internalized racial prejudice, which partially explains their initial reluctance to accept freedmen as citizens of their tribes with all of the rights of citizenship as persons who were "racially Indian."

The fact that Indianness had been racialized – meaning made into a racial category by whites –and was not merely a political identity, meant that even the adoption of the freedmen as citizens of the tribes would be insufficient to make them Indians because by the time the treaties of 1866 were executed, the status of being Indian had become primarily a racial identity, not a political one. Moreover, at the time of the 1866 treaties, the tribes had laws that prevented Indian tribal members from cohabitating with or marrying blacks. The laws, known as anti-miscegenation laws, were adopted by tribal leaders in order to protect individual Indian citizens from begetting offspring who would be deemed to have been corrupted by the presence of African blood, and therefore "Negro."[9]

As one federal court stated while reviewing a freedmen's appeal to be considered an Indian by blood, "one drop of African Blood taints the stream and makes it African in descent."[10] Hence federal law imposed the one-drop rule in determining whether former slaves with African and Indian ancestry could be considered "Indians by blood." One drop of African blood had the power of corrupting a person and transforming them into a "Negro" even when the majority of their ancestry or blood was Native American.[11] In light of federal law's interpretation of Indian identity, tribes enacted anti-miscegenation laws as a necessary form of self-preservation—a way to prevent the loss of tribal citizens since mixed race offspring with African ancestry would by law be assigned to the racial category of "Negro" not the racial category of Indian, and therefore would be forever lost from the tribe. The anti-miscegenation laws further entrenched the notion that black people were a people separate and apart from Indians and that no individual could occupy the dual status of black and Indian.

One of the first cases to define individual Indian identity in racialized terms was *United States v. Rogers,*[12] This case involved a white man, was indicted for the murder of another white man; the crime allegedly occurred in the Cherokee Nation. Rogers claimed that both he and his victim were Indian and, therefore, the circuit court lacked personal jurisdiction. Rogers based this claim on the fact that he had lived among the Cherokee Indians within the geographic boundaries of the tribe for many years, had married a Cherokee woman, and had children with her.

Furthermore, Rogers had renounced his United States citizenship and the Cherokee tribe adopted him as a full member, granting him all the rights and privileges of a natural-born Cherokee.

In interpreting the statute, the Court had to give meaning to Congress's use of "Indian." In doing so, the Court revealed its conception of Indian identity as a race, and not merely a political identity. The Court interpreted the Indian exception as "confined to those who by the usages and customs of the Indians are regarded as belonging to their race. It does not speak of members of a tribe, but of the race generally."[13] Without referencing the legislative history of the Act, or the meaning of the term "Indian" in other statutes, the Court held that Rogers was not "Indian" as that term was used in the statute. The Court stated that it was "very clear, that a white man who at mature age is adopted in an Indian tribe does not thereby become an Indian."[14] "Whatever obligations [Rogers] may have taken upon himself by becoming a Cherokee by adoption, his responsibility to the laws of the United States remained unchanged and undiminished. He was still a white man, of the white race, and therefore not within the exception in the act of Congress."[15] Thus, as early as 1846, the Supreme Court articulated a conception of "Indian" as a racial identity rather than one grounded in tribal membership. The Court thereby rejected the construct of Indian identity as a political identity in favor of a racial conception of Indian identity. This racialization of Indian people further destabilized tribal sovereignty by imposing an identity on indigenous people that they likely would not have chosen for themselves. In fact, the Court's opinion in Rogers suggests that the tribe had not chosen a racialized conception of "Indian," because it had adopted Rogers as a member of the "Indian family" despite the fact that he was racially "white."

Federal law has also defined "Indian" in racial terms by requiring a sufficient quantum of "Indian blood." Paul Spruhan, an expert in federal Indian law who has studied the blood quantum requirements extensively, found that the earliest use of blood quantum arose in the context of colonial law seeking to define the status of mixed-race individuals.[16] In 1866 Virginia extended blood quantum to define Indian as "every person, not a colored person, having one-fourth or more of Indian blood."[17] By the early twentieth century, Indians were beginning to think of themselves in racialized terms which is evident from the discourse of some tribal leaders who "themselves used the language of blood and descent to debate how to define [tribal] membership."[18]

The leadership of the Five Tribes understood the dominant society's racial ideology—that an individual's phenotype heavily influenced whites' willingness to perceive and accept an individual as Indian. They may also have understood that the surrounding states constructed black racial identity in terms of hypodescent, which meant that any known African ancestry could relegate an individual to the status of "Negro." Thus, Indians understood that mixing with blacks could have a corrupting effect on Indian identity and potentially destroy it. It was with this understanding that Indians adopted a preference for lighter skin and sought to protect Indian identity from the corrupting effects of blackness. One way to do this was through laws prohibiting race mixing between Indians and blacks. In the nineteenth century, the dominant social understanding of mixed-race children was that they inherited the status of the racially inferior parent.

The slaveholding tribes understood that the southern states surrounding them would classify an individual with Indian and Negro blood in accordance with state race-classification laws. This meant that the physical appearance of individual Indians could subject them to being classified as "Negro." Even in a post-slavery environment, Indians had an incentive to maintain racial distance between themselves and blacks to protect themselves from the indignities of Jim Crow. But why would Indian nations such as the Cherokees seek to distance themselves from blacks today when the one drop rule is no longer the law of the land and slavery and Jim Crow have been dismantled? Perhaps it is because blackness is still subordinated to other racial categories socially, and the tribes are trying to protect themselves from the subordinating effect of blackness.

In a brief filed with the federal appeals court, the Cherokees argued that only persons with federally documented Indian "blood" can be members of a federally recognized Indian tribe, and that therefore Indian blood is the essence of Indian identity. This argument is essentially an assertion that tribes are not competent to govern people who are deemed racially non-Indian. The Cherokees assert that the freedmen are a class of people who lack Indian blood, and therefore are not Indian. While some freedmen lack Indian ancestry, the reality is that the freedmen are not a homogenous group. Some freedmen do have Indian ancestry but the documentation of that ancestry was erased by law through the Dawes Commission's enrollment practices which excluded individuals from the "blood roll" of Indians if they were known to have African ancestry in addition to their Indian ancestry. If the goal of tribes is to strengthen tribal sovereignty and self-determination for indigenous people, tribes should never argue that they are incapable of governing people who lack Indian ancestry. Such an argument unnecessarily constrains tribal sovereignty and invites additional federally imposed restrictions on tribal sovereignty. The freedmen have had little success in the federal courts which generally opt to protect tribal sovereignty over African-Indian self-determination.

As a result of litigation proving fruitless, some freedman descendants are asking the federal government to recognize them as a separate and distinct tribe of people with all the rights of self-determination of a federally recognized Indian tribe. This strategy has little opportunity for success since the regulations defining the requirements for federal recognition impose cultural and historical requirements that the freedmen do not satisfy as a group. Because the freedmen have not had success vindicating their rights in federal court or through the other branches of the federal government, perhaps the next step is for them to seek the enforcement of their treaty rights in an international forum where early twentieth century notions of race no longer define the right to self-determination.

Although the US ceased entering treaties with Indian tribes in 1871,[19] many treaties that predated this time, including the post-Civil War treaties of 1866, remain in force as part of federal law, and define the federal government's relationship with tribes. In addition to these treaties, the federal government is now a party to the United Nations Declaration on the Rights of Indigenous Peoples.[20] Although this Declaration lacks the force of law, it provides strong guidance to nation states on the expectations of the international community with respect to the treatment of indigenous individuals and groups. The Declaration seeks to encourage nation states to work toward remedying the injustices that indigenous people continue to face as a result of conquest and colonialism. Article 2 of the Declaration provides that "Indigenous peoples and individuals are free and equal to all other peoples and individuals and have the right to be free from any kind of discrimination, in the exercise of their rights, in particular that based on their indigenous origin or identity."[21] This provision arguably protects the freedmen from discrimination by their own tribes, but only if they are "indigenous individuals." Because the tribes have determined that the freedmen are not citizens of the tribe and therefore are not Indian or "indigenous individuals," it will be difficult for the freedmen to invoke the protections of Article 2 of the Declaration. The problem with Article 2 of the Declaration is that it fails to recognize that some indigenous peoples, such as the freedmen, may suffer discrimination, not because of their indigenous identity, but because of their African ancestry, and that the discrimination may be practiced, not by the federal government or outsiders, but by the self- proclaimed indigenous individuals' own tribe.

Article 3 of the Declaration acknowledges that indigenous peoples have the right to self-determination and defines that right as guaranteeing indigenous people the right to "freely determine their political status and freely pursue their economic, social and cultural development."[22] This provision refers to indigenous "peoples" as a group and therefore would provide little assistance to the freedmen who lack the status of "indigenous peoples" due to the discriminatory determinations of their respective tribes. Article 6 of the Declaration provides that "every indigenous individual has the right to a nationality."[23] This provision arguably entitles the freedmen to recognition by their respective tribes, but it is not clear whether this provision was intended to apply only to nation states such as the US so as to entitle tribal members to US nationality.

The overarching problem with the UN Declaration from the freedmen's perspective is that it does not define "indigenous people or indigenous individuals." The UN Declaration assumes that indigenous people will be defined by indigenous groups in ways that reject the colonial influence of the conquering nation. What the UN Declaration overlooks is that some tribes have embraced colonial era doctrines defining Indian identity in determining who is an indigenous individual. Article 9 of the Declaration provides that indigenous "individuals have the right to belong to an indigenous community or nation, in accordance with the traditions and customs of the community or nation concerned. No discrimination of any kind may arise from the exercise of such a right."[24] This declaration suggests that not even indigenous tribes should be permitted to use a tribal membership framework that uses the race rules of the colonial era to discriminate against and exclude persons with indigenous ancestry from tribal membership simply because they also have African ancestry. The use of a racially discriminatory paradigm for determining tribal membership and its accompanying indigenous identity, is inconsistent with the Declaration on the Rights of Indigenous Peoples, and the International Convention on the Elimination of All Forms of Racial Discrimination.[25] The Declaration and the Convention create international norms with respect to the human rights of racial minorities and indigenous people. These international norms should be considered in resolving the freedmen descendants' status.

Presently, thousands of individual Americans self-identify as indigenous, but because they lack acceptance by a federally recognized Indian tribe, they have no means of having their indigenous identity recognized and legitimized by law. Such is the circumstance of the freedman descendants. Because their tribes have excluded them from tribal membership, they cannot claim an indigenous identity under federal or tribal law. Although it is not legally binding, the UN Declaration on the Rights of Indigenous Peoples stands as an important guide for not only the federal government, and the states, but also for tribes. Tribes that continue to define indigenous identity through rules that rely on racially discriminatory rolls created during the colonial era, perpetuate the maintenance of colonial era legal doctrine which operates to reinforce colonial power and maintain the subordination of all indigenous peoples.

ENDNOTES

1 There are five tribes that institutionalized slavery by law during the slavery era and after the Civil War entered into treaties with the federal government agreeing to end slavery and adopt their freed slaves as citizens of the tribe. Those five tribes are the Cherokee, Chickasaw, Creek, Choctaw and Seminole. Carla D. Pratt, Tribes and Tribulations: Beyond Sovereign Immunity and Toward Reparation and Reconciliation for the Estelusti, 11WASH AND LEE REAL L.J. 61 (2005).

2 For a discussion of the Cherokee's exclusion of the freedmen, see, http://www.nytimes.com/roomfordebate/2011/09/15/tribal-sovereignty-vs-racial-justice/slaverys-long-shadow

3 Santa Clara Pueblo v. Martinez, 436 U.S. 49 (1978).

4 Some provisions of the US Constitution are made applicable to Indian Tribes through federal legislation passed by Congress, known as the Indian Civil Rights Act (ICRA) 25 U.S.C. §1302 (1983).

5 Toll v. Moreno, 102 S. Ct. 2977, 2982 (2005); Arizona v. United States, No. 11–182 (S. Ct. June 25, 2012).

6 Tribal citizenship and tribal membership are used interchangeably herein.

7 417 U.S. 535 (1974).

8 Pratt, Tribes and Tribulations, supra note 1 at 96-103.

9 Carla D. Pratt, Loving Indian Style: Maintaining Racial Caste and Tribal Sovereignty Through Sexual Assimilation, 2007 WIS. L. REV. 409 (2007).

10 Miller v. Allen, 229 P. 152, 154 (Okla. 1924).

11 Id.

12 United States v. Rogers, 45 U.S. (4 How.) 567, 571 (1846).

13 Id. at 573.

14 Id. at 572-73.

15 Id. at 573.

16 See Paul Spruhan, A Legal History of Blood Quantum in Federal Indian Law, 51 S.D. L. REV. 5 (2006).

17 Id. (citing Act of Feb. 27, 1866, ch. 17, § 1, 1866 Va. Acts 84, 84).

18 Id. at 11 n.75.

19 Stephen L. Prevar, THE RIGHTS OF INDIANS AND TRIBES: THE AUTHORITATIVE ACLU GUIDE TO INDIAN AND TRIBAL RIGHTS, 27 (3d ed. 2002).

20 Despite initial reluctance to support the Declaration, the United States declared its support for the Declaration on December 16, 2010.

21 United Nations Declaration on the Rights of Indigenous Peoples, G. A. Res. 61/295, at 3, U.N. Doc. A/RES/61/295 (Oct. 2, 2007).

22 Id. at 4.

23 Id.

24 Id.

25 International Convention on the Elimination of All Forms of Racial Discrimination, G.A. Res. 2106 (XX) A, U.N. Doc. A/ RES/ 2106(XX) (December 21, 1965).

FRANCIS A. BOYLE was responsible for drafting the Biological Weapons Anti-Terrorism Act of 1989, the American implementing legislation for the 1972 Biological Weapons Convention.He served on the Board of Directors of Amnesty International (1988-1992), and represented Bosnia-Herzegovina at the World Court where he argued and won two World Court Orders for Bosnia on the basis of the 1948 Genocide Convention. He served as legal adviser to the Palestinian Delegation to the Middle East peace negotiations from 1991 to 1993. In 2007, he delivered the Bertrand Russell Peace Lectures. Professor Boyle teaches international law at the University of Illinois, Champaign and is author of, inter alia, The Future of International Law and American Foreign Policy, Foundations of World Order, The Criminality of Nuclear Deterrence, Palestine, Palestinians and International Law, Destroying World Order, Biowarfare & Terrorism, Tackling America's Toughest Questions, The Tamil Genocide by Sri Lanka and The Palestinian Right of Return Under International Law. He holds a Doctor of Law Magna Cum Laude as well as a Ph.D. in Political Science, both from Harvard University. He is a Member of the IHRAAM Directorate.

AFRICAN AMERICANS' RIGHT TO SELF-DETERMINATION

FRANCIS A. BOYLE

In order to commemorate the 500th anniversary of Columbus's invasion of the Americas, in early 1992 I was asked by the Organizers of the International Tribunal of Indigenous Peoples and Oppressed Nations in the U.S.A. to serve as Special Prosecutor of the United States of America for committing international crimes against Indigenous Peoples, People of Color, and Oppressed Nationalities, including and especially African Americans. For the purposes of these proceedings, the Organizers asked me to call African Americans the New Afrikan People.

The Tribunal was initiated by the American Indian Movement (AIM) with the support of representatives of the Puerto Rican People, the New Afrikan People, the Mexicano People, and "progressive White North Americans." Of course, I do not consider myself to be a "White North American." I was born Irish. During the past 840 years of resisting one of the most brutal and cruel colonial occupations in the history of humankind, we Irish know what the denial of self-determination, genocide, and gross violations of our most fundamental human rights are all about in our beloved Ireland and abroad, which atrocities still continue as of today.

In my capacity as Special Prosecutor of the United States Federal Government, I drew up an Indictment under international law that was

Francis A. Boyle (far left) on the floor of the World Court in 1993, just before he argued and then won the first of his two World Court Orders overwhelmingly in favor of Bosnia and Herzegovina on the basis of the 1948 Genocide Convention.

served upon the Attorney General of the United States and the United States Attorney in San Francisco prior to the convening of the Tribunal in that city just before "Columbus Day" on October 2-4, 1992 with a demand that they appear to defend the United States government from the charges.

I take it they saw no point in trying to defend the indefensible because no one showed up to defend the United States government, though they did publicly acknowledge receipt of our service of process. I will not go through all 37 charges of my Indictment here. But the proceedings of this pathbreaking International Tribunal have been recorded in a formal Verdict by the Tribunal; in a Video of the Tribunal; and in a Book on the Tribunal--all under the title *U.S.A. On Trial: The International Tribunal on Indigenous Peoples and Oppressed Nations in the United States.*

Six months after the conclusion of these San Francisco Tribunal proceedings, I was the Lawyer and Ambassador for the Republic of Bosnia and Herzegovina arguing its case for genocide against Yugoslavia before the International Court of Justice in The Hague, the World Court of the United Nations System. There I would singlehandedly win two World Court Orders overwhelmingly in favor of Bosnia against Yugoslavia to cease and desist from committing all acts of genocide against the Bosnians on 8 April 1993 and 13 September 1993. I treated the San Francisco Tribunal proceedings with as much care, attention, dignity, respect, and professionalism as I did the World Court proceedings for Bosnia. And the results were the same: massive, overwhelming, crushing victories for my clients in both the World Court and the San Francisco Tribunal!

For the purpose of this Conference, I want to briefly discuss the nine charges that I filed against the United States government for committing international crimes against African Americans. I believe that these nine charges succinctly state the fundamental principles of international law and human rights concerning African Americans. Obviously, these nine charges of my Indictment cannot answer all the questions African Americans might have with respect to their rights under international law and human rights law. But I do submit that these nine charges provide a solid foundation for providing guidance to African Americans as to their basic rights under international law that can be used in the future in order to navigate problems and issues as they arise to confront them today.

The Distinguished Judges composing this International Tribunal consisted of seven independent Experts on human rights drawn from all over the world. In their Verdict, Preliminary Findings, and Order of 4 October 1992, the Indigenous Peoples' Tribunal did not accept all of the 37 charges that I filed in my Indictment against the United States government for perpetrating international crimes against Indigenous Peoples, People of Color, and Oppressed Nations. But in their own words, the exact findings of this Tribunal on African Americans were as follows:

New Afrikans

7. With respect to the charges brought by the New Afrikan People, the Defendant, the Federal Government of the United States of America is, by unanimous vote, guilty as charged insofar as:

The Defendant has perpetrated the International Crime of Slavery upon the New Afrikan People as recognized in part by the 1926 Slavery Convention and the 1956 Supplementary Convention on the Abolition of Slavery, the Slave Trade, and Institutions and Practices Similar to Slavery.

The Defendant has perpetrated innumerable Crimes Against Humanity against the New Afrikan People as recognized by the Nuremberg Charter, Judgment, and Principles.

The Defendant has perpetrated the International Crime of Genocide against the New Afrikan People as recognized by the 1948 Genocide Convention.

The Defendant has perpetrated the International Crime of Apartheid against the New Afrikan People as recognized by the 1973 Apartheid Convention.

The Defendant has perpetrated a gross and consistent pattern of violations of the most fundamental human rights of the New Afrikan People as recognized by the 1948 Universal Declaration of Human Rights and the two United Nations Human Rights Covenants of 1966.

The Defendant has perpetrated a gross and consistent pattern of violations of the 1965 Racism Convention against the New Afrikan People. *The Defendant is the paradigmatic example of an irremediably racist state in international relations today.* (my emphasis added)

The Defendant has denied and violated the international legal right of the New Afrikan People to self-determination as recognized by the United Nations Charter, the two United Nations Human Rights Covenants of 1966, customary international law, and jus cogens.

[Let me repeat that: By unanimous vote, Ibid.]

The Defendant has illegally refused to accord full-scope protections as Prisoners-of-War to captured New Afrikan independence fighters in violation of the Third Geneva Convention of 1949 and Additional Protocol I thereto of 1977. The Defendant's treatment of captured New Afrikan independence fighters as "common criminals" and "terrorists" constitutes a "grave breach" of the Geneva Accords and thus a serious war crime.

Additional Findings

11. In light of the foregoing findings, this Tribunal also, by unanimous vote, finds the Defendant guilty as charged in paragraph 37, which, as amended, reads:

In light of the foregoing international crimes, the Defendant constitutes a Criminal Conspiracy and a Criminal Organization in accordance with the Nuremberg Charter, Judgment, and Principles and the other sources of public international law specified above, and the Federal Government of the United States of America is similar to the Nazi government of World War II Germany.

[This powerful Finding speaks for itself and requires no explanation by me.]

....

13. With respect to the following charges brought by the New African People:

a. four members of the Tribunal find the Defendant guilty as charged in paragraph 11, which, as amended, reads:

The Defendant has illegally refused to pay reparations to the New Afrikan People for the commission of the International Crime of Slavery against Them in violation of basic norms of customary international law requiring such reparations to be paid.

Three members of the Tribunal reserve the right to consider the documentary evidence further before making a final determination.

[In all honesty, I do not know what more evidence these three members of the Tribunal wanted to see before they were willing to order that the United States government must pay reparations for slavery to

African Americans—with all due respect to these three Judges. To the best of my knowledge, this was the first time ever that any Lawyer had argued in favor of reparations for slavery for African Americans before an International Tribunal. A 4 in favor to 0 against to 3 abstentions Verdict was not a bad outcome for the first time through, though it was disappointing to me personally—it should have been unanimous. I and others lawyers will have to learn from this experience in order to do a better job the next time around on this critical issue of obtaining Reparations for Slavery to African Americans. But in retrospect, however, I should have argued to the San Francisco Trubunal that African Americans today suffer from intergenerational post-traumatic stress disorder (P.T.S.D.) in order to drive home to the Judges the direct and immediate deleterious and debilitating effects that Slavery still now afflicts upon African Americans personally and as a People with a right of self-determination.]

b. Three members of the Tribunal find the Defendant guilty as charged in paragraph 18, which reads:

The Defendant has illegally refused to apply the United Nations Decolonization Resolution of 1960 to the New Afrikan People and to the Territories that they principally inhabit. Pursuant thereto, the Defendant has an absolute international legal obligation to decolonize New Afrikan Territories immediately and to transfer all powers it currently exercises there to the New Afrikan People.

Four members of the Tribunal reserve the right to consider the documentary evidence further before making a final determination.

Obviously, I lost this Land "Reparations" argument by 3 in favor to 0 against to 4 abstaining. The Organizers of the San Francisco Tribunal had requested me to argue for this Land "Reparations" form of relief for African Americans, and I did that to the best of my ability. I suspect it appeared to be too "radical" a proposition for a majority of Judges on the Tribunal to endorse. But I take some consolation from the fact that at least three Judges agreed with me and none dissented.

The Tribunal concluded its Verdict with the following Order to the United States government: "Now therefore, it is ordered, adjudged and decreed that the Defendant cease and desist from the commission of the crimes it has been found guilty of herein." Pursuant thereto, I then filed a copy of this San Francisco Verdict with its Cease and Desist Order upon the Attorney General of the United States of America in Washington, D.C.

In return, I later received a 5 February 1993 Letter from the U.S. Department of Justice that acknowledged the receipt of the San Francisco Tribunal Verdict and its Cease and Desist Order against the United States government. This U.S. D.O.J Letter then advised me: "If you, or the Tribunal, have any evidence of the violation of federal criminal law, we ask that you provide that information to your local office of the Federal Bureau of Investigation."

As I saw it at the time, and still see it as of today, historically this would be analogous to the Nazi Ministry of "Justice" advising a German lawyer representing the Jews to file his Complaint of criminal law violations by the Nazi government against the Jews with the Gestapo. The F.B.I is and has always been the American Gestapo—especially for all Peoples of Color living within its imperial domain, and in particular against African Americans. [1] I also make that statement on the basis of first-hand personal experience.

In the summer of 2004 the F.B.I. and the C.I.A/F.B.I Joint Terrorist Task Force in Springfield, Illinois put me on all of the U.S. government's so-called "terrorist watch lists" because I refused to become an informant for them against my Arab and Muslim Clients, which would have violated their Constitutional Rights and my Ethical Obligation as an attorney. That is what the U.S. government's "war on terrorism" is really all about: It is a War by the White Racist Judeo-Christian Financial Power Elite of America against Arabs and Muslims—many of whom are African Americans—both in this country and abroad. The Crusades all over again!

As Special Prosecutor for the San Francisco Tribunal, it came as no surprise to me that the Judges unanimously endorsed most of my charges against the United States government with respect to African Americans. This is because the principles of international law with respect to African Americans are incontestable, and thus so glaringly obvious for the entire world to see. I most respectfully submit that African Americans should use the Tribunal's Verdict, Preliminary Findings, and Order in order to support, promote, and defend their basic rights under international law, including and especially African Americans' right to self-determination as found unanimously by the San Francisco Tribunal in 1992.

In this regard, the Verdict, Preliminary Findings, and Order of this San Francisco Tribunal qualify as a "judicial decision" within the meaning of Article 38(1)(d) of the Statute of the International Court of Justice. Pursuant thereto, this Verdict, Preliminary Findings, and Order constitute "subsidiary means for the determination of rules of law" for international law and practice. Furthermore, the Statute of the International Court of Justice is an "integral part" of the United Nations Charter under Article 92 thereof. Hence the San Francisco Tribunal's Verdict, Preliminary Findings, and Order can be relied upon by the International Court of Justice itself, by the International Criminal Court, by some other International Tribunal, or by any other Court in the world today, as well as by any People or State of the World Community—including and especially by African Americans. The Verdict of the San Francisco Tribunal still serves as adequate notice to the appropriate officials in the United States Federal Government that they bear personal criminal responsibility under international law and the domestic legal systems of all Peoples and States in the World Community for designing and implementing these illegal, criminal and reprehensible policies and practices against Indigenous Peoples and Peoples of Color living in North America, including and especially against African Americans.

Obviously, in my brief presentation here today, I do not have the time to go through each and every one of these nine charges; to discuss all of the factual evidence that supported these nine charges; or to provide you with an analysis of the international legal bases for each one of these nine charges. For that type of information, I refer you to the Video and the Book on the San Francisco Tribunal as well as to its Verdict, Preliminary Findings, and Order itself. But in the discussions that follow tonight and tomorrow, I will be happy to respond to any questions you might have.

ENDNOTES

1 See M. Wesley Swearingen, FBI Secrets: An Agent's Expose (1995).

PANEL THREE

COLLECTIVE EMPOWERMENT INSTITUTIONS, JURISDICTIONS...

- Are African Americans a people?
- Do they want a collective future or do they want to assimilate?
- Should African Americans conduct a national plebiscite to help identify/implement their collective aspirations?
- Should they establish a Constituent Assembly to speak for them and operate in collaboration with other levels of US government?
- Would some governmental institutions or jurisdictions that directly impact African American communities be more effective if under African American control?
- Should they seek a share of their own federal/state tax dollars?
- Might such ideas, if constitutionally empowered, be viewed as the logical goals of a comprehensive reparations movement?

Left to right: Speakers Henry English, Dr. John Boyd, Atty. Choke Lumumba, Dr. Farid I. Muhammad. Moderator, Kamm Howard.

FARID I. MUHAMMAD was born, raised and educated in Harlem, N.Y.C. He currently serves as the Chairman of the Department of Behavioral Sciences at East-West University (EWU) in Chicago. He holds a M.A. in Clinical Psychology (Bradley University) and an Ed.D. in Administration & Management (University of Sarasota / Argosy) in Florida. He served as Director of the Ministry of Education for the Muhammad University of Islam/Sister Clara Muhammad school system Chicago, Illinois 1975-1979. While at EWU he also designed and managed multi-million dollar federal projects under the U.S. Department of Education designed to help identify and train qualified first-generation and low-income high school students who needed socio-academic assistance in making a transition to varied institutions of higher education. Dr. Muhammad works in collaboration with the Organization of Islamic Cooperation (OIC), a confederation of 57 Muslim Nations of the UN and serves as a member of the Board of Trustees (BOT) of the American Islamic College (AIC).He also serves as a member of the Directorate of the International Human Rights Association of American Minorities (IHRAAM). Dr. Muhammad has represented IHRAAM in a variety of international and domestic venues, including heading a 41 member delegation to the UN/WCAR in Durban, South Africa 2001. His international travels include visits to Africa, Canada, the Caribbean, Europe and the Middle-East.

NATIONAL SURVEY ON AFRICAN AMERICAN SELF-DETERMINATION

FARID I. MUHAMMAD

Distinguished co-members of the Panel, honored guests, dear brothers and sisters; it is a distinct privilege to help address the challenging issues suggested by the title of this unique panel. Without question, the theme "Collective Empowerment" poses an array of questions that can no longer be ignored by the African-American leadership. As noted in the Conference program such a title might logically raise questions such as: Do Peoples of African Descent in the USA want a collective future or do they want to assimilate? Should African-Americans conduct a national plebiscite to help identify and implement their collective aspirations? Should they develop a Constituent Assembly to speak for them and operate in collaboration with other levels of the US Government? These are among the more critical and operationally relevant issues that will hopefully be explored by this distinguished panel.

As a member of the IHRAAM Directorate and facilitator of the research team which conducted a national survey of the African-American Community relative to the central theme of "**African-American Self-Determination**", we thought this might be an ideal occasion to formally share an outline of our core findings. However, it is important that we first consider this exploratory study within its appropriate social, legal, historical, and international context.

Ever since the unprecedented January 16, 1995 report submitted to the then UN Commission on Human Rights as prepared by UN Special Rapporteur Maurice Glélé-Ahanhanzo,[1] very little research has been done which is properly nuanced to assess the legitimate human rights concerns of American national minorities. This is particularly true relative to the unique problems confronted by the formerly enslaved ethnic minority population of African-Americans. Within the framework of international law, this now historic study focused on assessing contemporary forms of racism, racial discrimination, xenophobia, and related intolerance in the U.S.A.

As was amply evidenced in this historic report, gross disparities between the majority European-American and African-American communities relative to such critical socio-economic indicators as: health, education, housing, employment, political participation, economic development, criminal justice and the application of the death penalty, police violence and incitement to racial hatred are well documented and continue to worsen.[2]

It was within this socio-legal context that the International Human Rights Association of American Minorities (IHRAAM) conducted a national telephone survey of predominantly African-American citizens throughout the U.S.A. This exploratory study was conducted in May, 1999 and involved a modest survey sample of 710 subjects covering 24 major American cities with high concentrations of African-American voters. The primary purpose of this fledging study was to help generate much needed basal data relative to assessing African-Americans citizens' familiarity with human rights provisions as covered under international law, as well as determining their attitude toward the issue of "**Self-Determination**". Except for a pilot phone survey of registered voters in the City of Chicago, as conducted by IHRAAM in 1993, comparable data is almost non-existent.

It was hypothesized that the socio-political attitudes held by African-Americans, relative to the issue of **"Self-Determination",** can be explained by the life experiences of such citizens. There were seven variables explored in relations to such citizen attitudes. They were: (1) voter registration status; (2) gender; (3) level of education; (4) age; (5) social status; (6) race/ethnicity; and (7) geographic region of the country.

Methodology and Treatment of Data

The U.S. Bureau of Census reported that as of 1990 there were in excess of 31 million African-Americans who comprised 12.4% of the American population at that time. Using Census Bureau criteria, 24 key American cities were systematically selected as a function of their: size (being rated large, midsize and smaller metropolitan statistical areas

SMA's), being part of demographic clusters with high concentrations of African-Americans, and being geographically reflective of the varied regions of the U.S.A. where African-Americans are proportionally represented (i.e. east, south, central and western regions).

In descending order of their proportional representation of 710 subjects subsequently identified and selected for this survey, the following are the 24 cities selected as the target population area for study: New York City, NY (all 5 boroughs); Chicago, IL; Detroit, MI; Atlanta, GA; Los Angeles, CA; Cleveland, OH; Baton Rouge, LA; Oakland, CA; Jackson, MS; Fayetteville, NC; Richmond, VA; Louisville, KY; Seattle, WA; Florence, SC; Nashville, TN; Las Vegas, NV; Tuscaloosa, AL; Longview, TX; Fort Pierce, FL; Pine Bluff, AR; Atlantic City, NJ; Lawton, TX; Pascagouola, MS; and South Bend, IN.

Similarly, using U.S. Census data and computer accessed listings of residential phone numbers (by zip codes) within each of these targeted communities which had the highest proportions of African-American citizens, all subjects were selected using standard systematic sampling procedures. Subjects were uniformly called and interviewed using a uniform questionnaire consisting of fourteen items. Though this initial sample was relatively small there was a high degree of precision and thoroughness in the sampling procedures and data collection process. The data were statistically robust and reflective of the demographic and proportional representation noted in aggregate U.S. Census data.

Survey items 1-10 assessed each subject's information relative to their respective social characteristics (i.e. age, gender, education, social status, etc.). Subjects' responses to survey items 11-13 inclusive were averaged and generated a composite score. These items dealt with their opinions concerning "**Group Rights",** creation of a "**National Assembly**", and the issue of independent control over local institutions and community services. Composite scores ranged from **+ 3.00 (high self-determination)** to **-3.00 (low self-determination**). This "Self-Determination" index was then statistically analyzed as a function of the seven subject variables mentioned earlier (i.e. age, gender, race/ ethnicity, etc).

Appropriate statistical analyses of the survey data were performed. This treatment of the data was done to test for possible significant differences and/or correlations between subjects' voter registration status, gender, level of education, age, social status, race/ ethnicity, and geographic region; and their general awareness of the socio-legal options afforded by international human rights law and attitudes toward the issue of "self-determination" for African-Americans. Additionally, a regression analysis of the survey data was performed to identify which of the above variables or combination of variables, were best "predictors" of citizens' attitudes toward the issue of "self-determination".

Results and Conclusion

The seven subject variables were explored in relation to citizen awareness and attitude scores. A profile of subject characteristics revealed the following: 90% of those surveyed were born in the U.S.A. while 10% came from other countries; 91% were registered voters while 9% were not; only 39% were male while 61% were female; 21% had not completed high school, 34% were high school graduates, 24% had completed some college, 9% were college graduates and 12% had some level of post-collegiate study. Subjects' ages ranged from 18 - 65+ years of age, while 77% reported living in "blue-collar/working-class" communities and 23% claimed to reside in "white-collar/ professional-class" neighborhoods. It was noted that 76% of those surveyed were African-Americans, 11% were European-Americans, and 13% were of other racial/ethnic backgrounds. Finally, results indicated that 29% of those surveyed resided in the Eastern Regions of the U.S.A, 25% in the Southern States, 33% in the Central Region, and 13% in the Western Region. All data were subject to thorough statistical analyses.

Several subject variables were proved to be significantly related to the attitudes expressed regarding "Self-Determination". In short, a regression analysis of the data revealed that the singularly most potent predictor of "positive" citizen attitudes toward this issue was "race/ ethnicity". It was found that African-Americans citizens, in aggregate, who have "college level" training, live in "blue-collar/working class" neighborhoods, and who are "registered voters"; demonstrate the statistically **strongest desire** to have their "collective rights" recognized, create an independent National Assembly to represent their common interests, and to "exert independent control over those institutions and services that most directly affect their own communities". Conversely, "Non-African-American" citizens, as a group, and those who were not "native-born", live in the Southern Region of the U.S.A., and are over 65+ years of age; represent those who are statistically far **less supportive** of these goals.

It was found that 67% of all African-Americans surveyed felt that "African-American voters should participate in an independent election to create a **National Assembly** to help monitor and represent their own collective interests". When asked if they would be in favor of "having some degree of independent control over those institutions and services that most directly affect their own communities", 81% of all African-Americans said "yes", only 9% were "uncertain" and 10%

responded "no". The composite measure of "Self-Determination" (items # 11-13 inclusive) revealed that 75.07% of all respondents and 80.16% of African-Americans were in the "support range" of "Self-Determination" for African-Americans, while 16.91% of all subjects were "non-supportive" and 8.02% were in the range of "uncertainty".

A detailed visual profile of the percentage of responses to the survey questions comprising the composite measure of "Self-Determination" (items # 11-13) are represented in the following power-point diagrams. A summary of the results of the regression analysis/ statistics, which depict the best social predictors of "Self-Determination", are likewise presented in Figure 3.

In 2001 a more comprehensive version of this study was shared by IHRAAM with the UN Human Rights Commission, the UN/World Conference on Racism (Durban, South Africa), as well as the UN Special Working Group on Minorities. In conclusion, it is highly recommended that further and more thorough investigative studies of this nature be conducted to methodically assess the needs, concerns and socio-political aspirations of the African-American and similarly marginalized national minorities in the U.S.A. Such research, which is simultaneously framed within the context of international human right laws and provisions, is deemed essential as we strive to address the long-term challenges posed by this auspicious Conference and noteworthy panel.

QUESTION 11

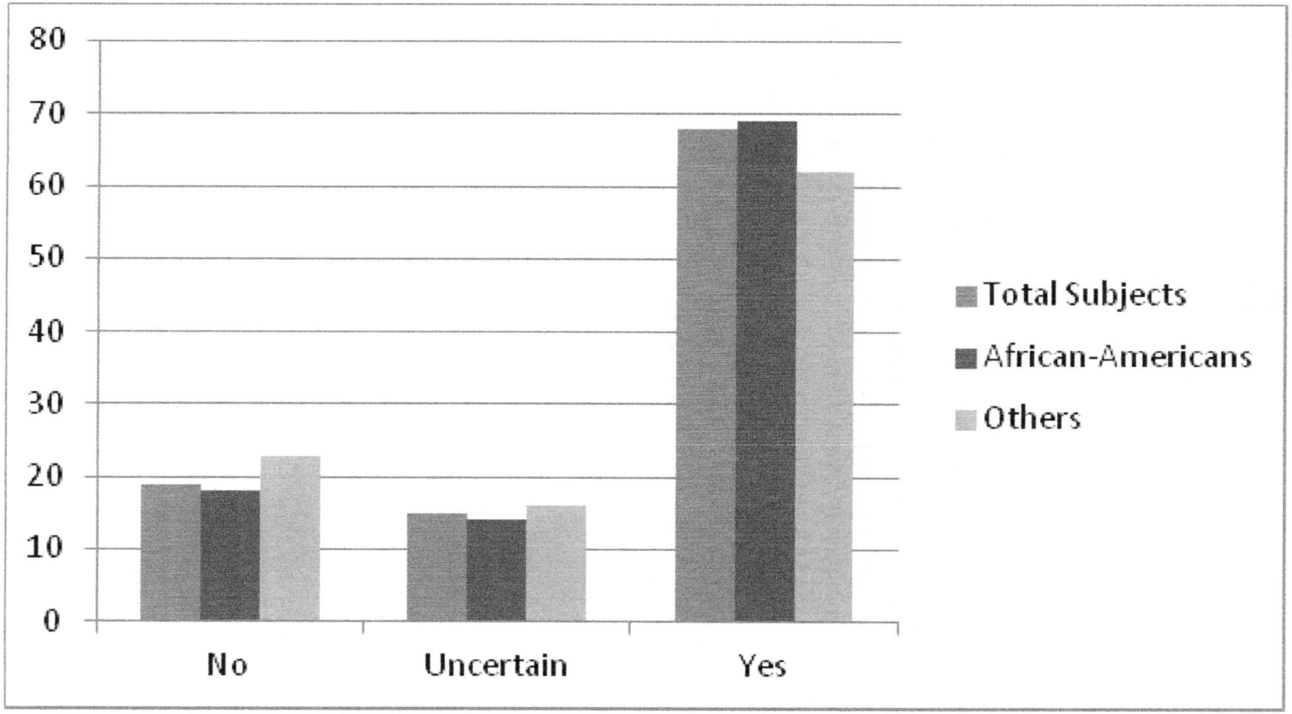

Do you believe that in certain instances African-Americans have the right to be treated as a “collective body”, and not just as “individuals”, in the attempt to address their common problems and needs?

QUESTION 12

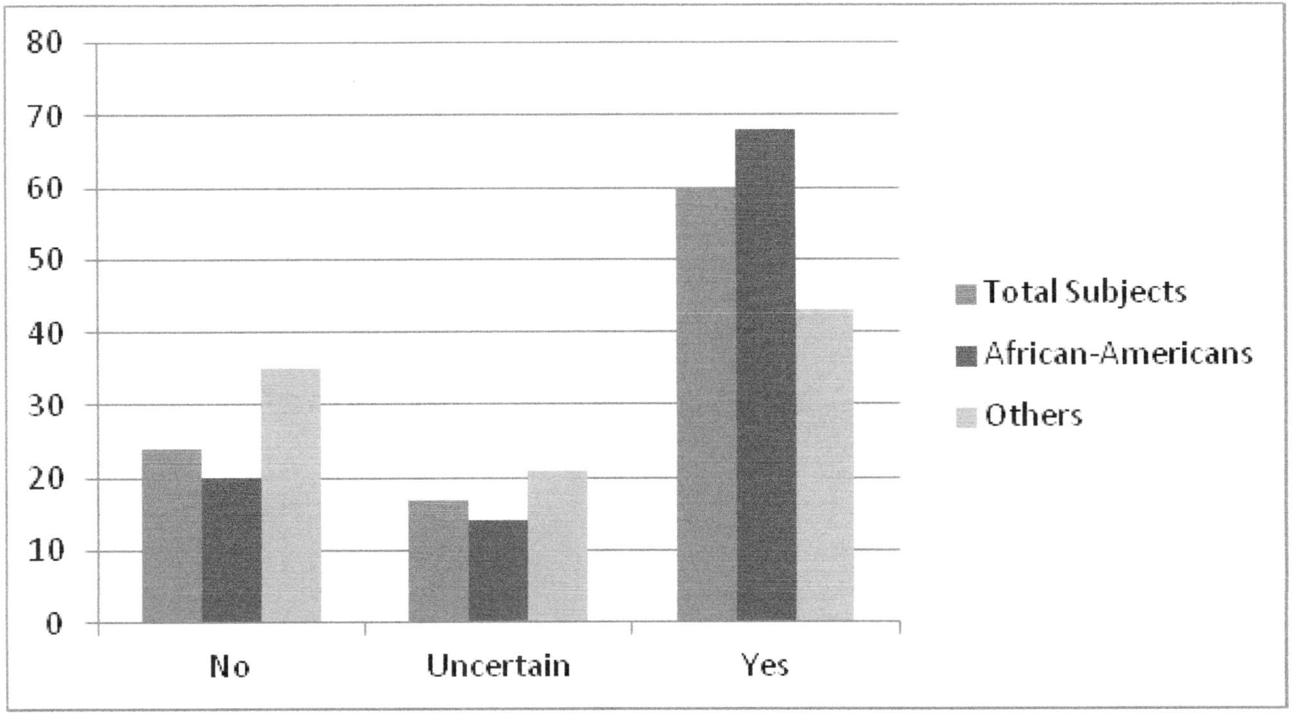

If presented with the opportunity, should African-American voters participate in an independent election to create a "National Assembly" to help monitor and represent their own collective interest?

QUESTION 13

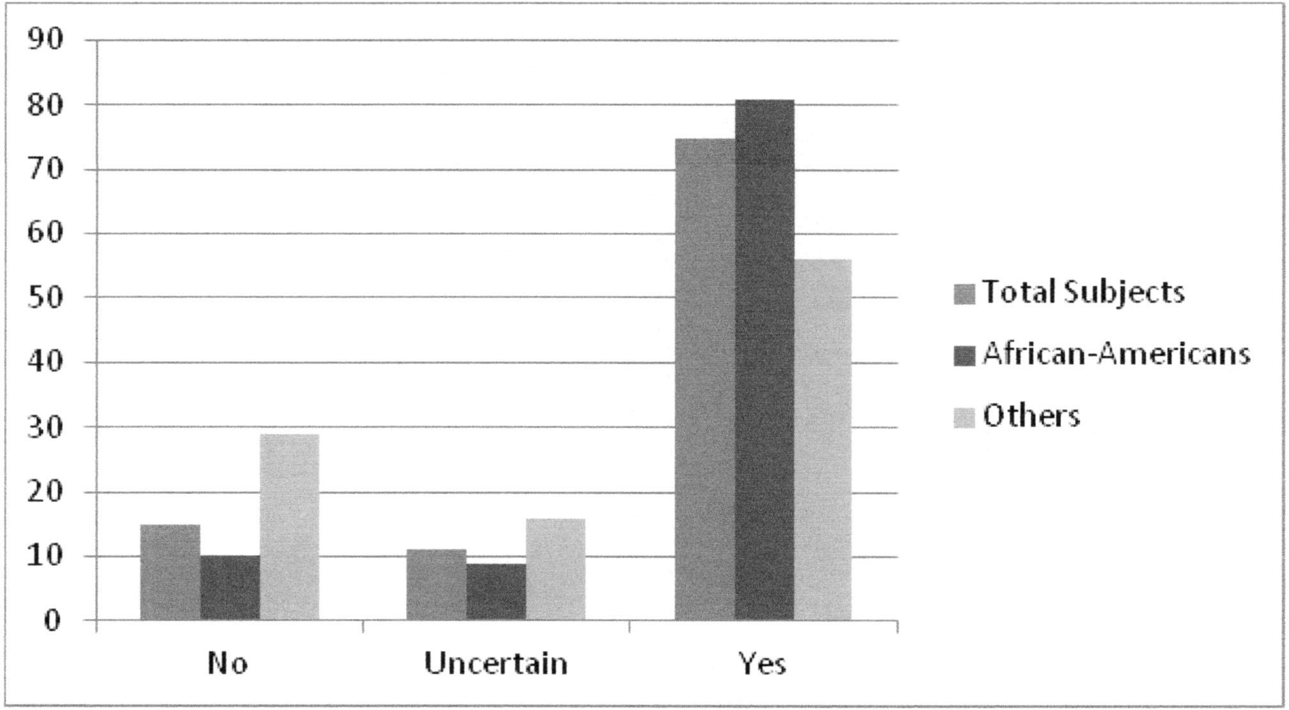

Would you be in favor of African-American having some degree of independent control over those institutions and services that most directly affect their own communities?

Self-Determination

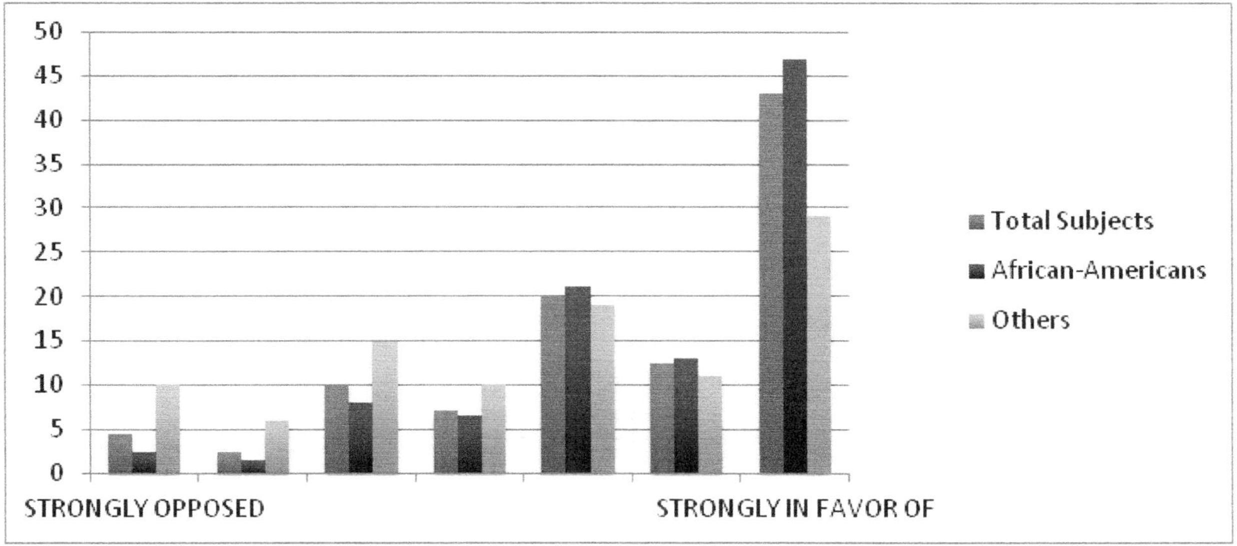

-3.00 Composite Scores +3.00

Over-All Self-Determination Scores

REGRESSION STATISTICS	
Multiple R	0.264361267
R Square	0.006988688
Adjusted R Square	0.058895882
Standard Error	1.685375861
Observations	686

anova					
REGRESSION	6	144.4914288	18.0614288	6.358556865	5.66E-08
Residual	677	1923.012944	2.840491794		
Total	685	2067.504373			

variable	coefficiants	standard error		P-Value	lower 95%	upper 95%	lower 95%	upper 95%
intercept	2.990108515	0.566482494	5.27837761	1.76E-07	1.877836151	4.102380879	1.877836151	4.102380879
RACE	-0.185733531	0.045749244	-405981638	0.000055	-275560879	-0.095906183	-0.275560879	-0.095906183
GRADE	-0.098881947	0.042630234	-2.319526277	0.02066314	-0.182585205	-0.015178888	-0.182585205	-0.015178888
NEIGHBOR	-0.35072543	0.15204712	-2.306689062	0.021373178	-0.649265653	-0.052185207	-0.649265853	-0.052185207
REGISTERED	-0.53226929	0.147596331	-2.149746271	0.031928931	-1.018417687	-0.046120892	-1.018417887	-0.048120892
GENDER	0.233241581	0.132381896	1.762150501	0.078495098	-0.02664726	0.493130422	-0.02884726	0.493130422
AGE	-0.087480758	0.055698	-1.57062655	0.116736647	-0.196842208	0.021880691	-0.196842208	0.021880691
REGION	0.087512434	0.065937401	1.327204788	0.184888358	-0.041953788	0.216978657	-0.041953788	0.216978657
CITIZEN	-0.050530083	0.243152294	-0.207812488	0.835437879	-0.527952738	0.426892572	-0.527952738	0.426892572

BEST PREDICTORS OF SELF DETERMINATION

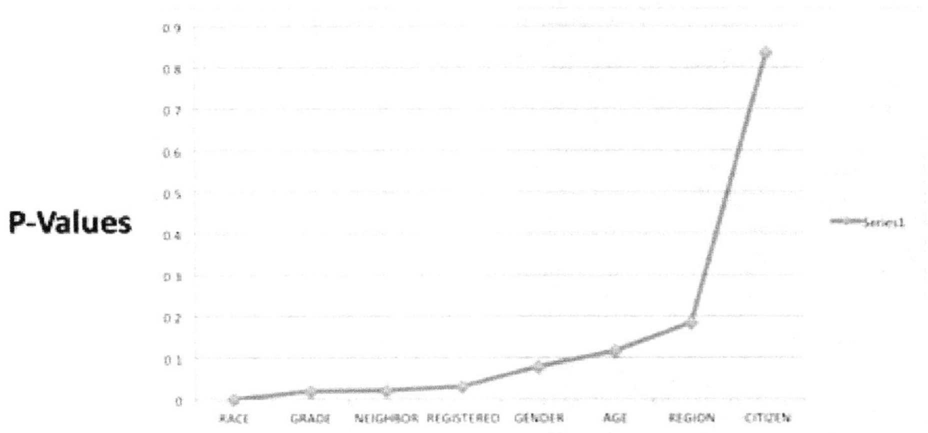

FIGURE 3: REGRESSION ANALYSIS OF SUBJECT VARIABLES

Attorney Chokwe Lumumba is the National Chairman and a cofounder of the New Afrikan People's Organization (N.A.P.O.) and has served as chairperson since its inception in 1984 having been re-elected to the position in 2004. On July 7, 2009, Chokwe Lumumba was seated as Ward 2 City Councilperson in Jackson, MS. He has pursued human rights on the streets and in the courtroom. He graduated with honors from Wayne State University Law School in 1975 after finishing first in his Freshman law class in 1973-74. In 1977, Chokwe Lumumba briefly served as Attorney for Black Liberation Army Soldier, Assata Shakur, in a murder case which was dismissed in Brooklyn, New York. Practicing law for more than 35 years, Lumumba is currently the senior law partner of Lumumba, Freelon and Associates in Jackson, MS.

DO WE NEED SELF-DETERMINING INSTITUTIONS?

Chokwe Lumumba

I'm delighted to be here and share some time with you. I have always been an admirer of the work IHRAAM has been doing. In fact I think I was around when they first started doing some of this work. I bring greetings not only from the New Afrikan Peoples Organization and Malcolm X Grassroots Movement, but I can now speak for Ward 2 of Jackson, Mississippi. From my brothers and sisters from Jackson, Mississippi and most importantly from my own family, I bring greetings.

This is a wonderful work and wonderful question that is raised here. At the outset, we should understand that the election of Barack Obama is what we might call a quintessential victory for the civil rights movement. It is the quintessential victory for those that worked so hard and had to start at white-only counters, white-only restrooms, and white-only water fountains and had to face the years of lynching and things of that nature. It's amazing to see that our mothers, our fathers, our grandmothers, our grandfathers went through that terrible history of Jim Crow and American apartheid. So the achievement of that election is a quintessential, and to some extent, still symbolic but still to some extent, a victory for the civil rights movement nonetheless.

But then we have to understand what Malcolm tells us. He pointed out to us that civil rights are different than human rights. Civil rights are what they gave you and human rights are what you always had. And that a victory for the civil rights movement is not necessarily a victory in the human rights movement. If we do not direct it in that direction and we allow things to be loosely interpreted, sloppily interpreted, and misinterpreted, then what we will find is that the quintessential victory of the civil rights movements actually winds up being a defeat in the human rights movement.

Because what it does is serve as window dressing in order to conceal the abuses which still take place. We have had problems ever since we were snatched from the coast of Africa. You've been in war for a long time. You may have not been *at* war for very long, but you certainly have been *in* war for a long time. You were in war ever since they snatched our ancestors from the African Continent. And to address that war and to have some kind of conceptual understanding of that war is very important. Because if we don't, we won't understand what a victory is and what a defeat is, and how to distinguish between the two. The reality is that our problems did not start with not being able to go to the same bathroom as white folks, that's not where our problems started. Problems started when our self-determination was snatched from us and when we were unable to make decisions which we had made for centuries by ourselves. We lost the ability to control our legacy and our wealth and to hand it down to generations that came after us. And so that is why so many of us have come here today from various different movements dealing with the question of self-determination, and dealing with the question of reparations because we understand that the human rights victory has not been achieved.

The human rights victory, unlike the civil rights victory, is revolutionary. Victory in the human rights concept requires a revolution. A victory in the civil rights concept requires certain modifications of perceptions over a period of time. But victory in human rights where people who have lost the ability to govern themselves, and then regain power over themselves is revolutionary because those other people in power don't give away power. They don't just say you can have your power back. And so in order to get that power back you have to find economic, political, and social ways to take that power back, not their power, but the power that belongs to you. So this is what we talk about when we address this important and interesting question.

I'm going to focus on a couple of key concepts and then move on. I'm a not a technician of international litigation of human rights law. As busy as I've been, I've never had the opportunity to get a technical understanding of the various different covenants. Of course, I've studied the covenants and some of the international conventions and I definitely have an understanding of the international law concept. But what we are being introduced to today by the National Conference by Black Lawyers, by people like Standish Willis, and what we have been introduced to for some time by organizations like IHRAAM, is the idea of using these covenants and things of the technical aspect to understand them, and understand how we must utilize them in order to bring our struggle to the international view of the world.

Malcolm told us that. Malcolm said that you really look kinda stupid—I know he didn't really put it like that, but knowing Malcolm he probably would put it pretty close to that—he said you look pretty stupid when instead of taking the criminal to court, you go to court and the criminal is in charge of the court! So what he says is that you need to find a way in order to take it to the international level. Malcolm was living at a time when the world was changing in terms of the United Nations. African nations, Latin American nations, Middle Eastern nations, were having revolutions and they were introducing into the General Assembly of the United Nations progressive nations who would go on to make different kinds of conventions and different types of decisions which would develop international law related to the non-self governing territories and upon the self-determination rights of territories. They would begin to expand that, whereas the initial United Nations was really pretty much controlled by the people who were the problem.

Right now we are back in the situation where the United Nations is pretty much controlled by the people who are the problem because of the grip that the Security Council has on the United Nations. So we have to be innovative in relation to the United Nations as an arena, as a stream, where we can introduce some of our concepts and try to educate the world. Where we can use whatever modalities we have and which we can find in order to progress our struggle. But we cannot become reliant upon it totally. We have to understand that the power ultimately comes from the people. And only the people will move us forward. Not only the people here, but the people around the world. Like Martin Luther King said, "Injustice anywhere is a threat to justice everywhere."

So we can't sit around here crying about Trayvon Martin if we did not say anything about those people in Afghanistan who got butchered by the American military. We have to understand. We have to have an understanding of, and partially an answer to this question that we ask ourselves: do we need independent or self-determining organs in order to try to make our decisions.

Martin Luther King said towards the end of his life, according to Harry Belafonte, that "We are going to win this integration thing, but I am getting a little leery about it. Seems like we are integrating into a burning house." So he was not impressed by the way that America treated those that were accepted as American. And he could not be sure that they would treat us in the proper way. Of course he was prophetic in that regard. As we found out, before he died he embraced the poor people's march, he embraced the various different economic modalities which were necessary to contest the power of the United States capitalist giant that was suppressing the power of not only Africans, but suppressing the power of all types of people all over the country. Martin Luther King was a prophet in the respect that here we sit, supposedly integrated into the country, and we do not have a pot to pee in, so to speak. We are getting worse off than we were. The people on Occupy Wall Street talked about the 99%. We must be 199 % because when everyone else is catching hell, we are catching super hell. We are in bad shape. And we see this all over the country.

It was a very proud experience when we busted out in various different places: in Chicago with the experience of the election Harold Washington; in Detroit when we took over the city council, we took over the mayoralty and we had 30 judges and out of the 30 judges that were adjudicating in Detroit, Michigan, we wound up with 25 that were black and two of them were white guys that said that they were communists and supported the black folks. So this is legal revolutionary black work. And we had this all over the country. But all of those things are being ruined. Gentrification has been the weapon which has wiped us out in city after city: in Washington, DC, in Harlem, NY, and right now working on Detroit, Michigan. And it has gotten a crazy man in office here in Chicago.

These are the kinds of problems we have. We shouldn't have to face these problems in 2012 if in fact a movement is a progression which is assured. But a movement is only assured in a progressive manner if the people make it that way. We cannot lay down on the job. We must understand that time never stands still. We must understand that nothing ever stands still. So either we are getting better or we are getting worse. And what has been happening over the last decade and several decades is that we have been getting worse. So we have to take a clear look at this self-determination thing and see how much interest we have in it and how much importance it has to us.

It's not only import from a political perspective, so we can say a dark guy is the mayor or a dark guy is the sheriff and things of that nature, but it is important to us from an economic perspective. It has to make a difference in our people's lives. When we elect these governmental officials that look like us and who don't make any difference in our lives, then we have to start taking a look at what officials we are electing. And one of things we have to do is we have to give them a litmus test. We have to ask them: "What do you know about these questions that the brothers have asked here today? What do you know about this self-determination thing? What is your position on self-determination? Are you just one of those people that feel that they should be elected because God has ordained you and you are going to be alright, in other words are nothing but a social opportunist? If you do not have a viewpoint which can be expressed on a sheet of paper, other than talking about you and where you were born and where you are going and all that kind of stuff, then you got a problem."

So we need predictable people that we put into office. One of the things that needs to be predictable about them is their view about self-determination. I think the answer to the question is obviously that we have to have self-determination. That we have to be identified as a group of people, not just because it is something fashionable, but because you do not get power unless you operate as a group of people. You do not get economic power unless you operate as a group of people. You do not get political power unless you act as a group of people. So it is very important that we combine together and operate as a group. And one of the main reasons it is important is because we *are* a people. Just because you go around barking all the time does not mean you are not a cat. If you're a cat you're cat, if you're a dog, you're a dog.

And what we are is Africans, that's what we are. We are Africans. We are different types of Africans from different parts of the world and different cultural experiences that has brought us to different places, but we are still essentially African. And one of the reasons we are still essentially African is because of the horrific history of the United States which refused to allow us—the combination of people—to create a society which could in fact be considered some kind of integrated society. Secondly, the way that our introduction to this continent came about was a problem. It's a problem to take people into slavery, to put us here and to keep us on the bottom. And then integration became our great grandmother or aunt working in some white man's house—that's what integration was. Raising his kids, and scrubbing his floors and things of that nature. That's not the kind of integration we're looking for. We're looking for the qualitative resurrection for us as a people and as a people of power.

I think that the answer to the question is yes, we have to be identified as a people. We've always had this name problem, this identity problem. We were Negros at one point. We were colored folks at one point. It's interesting because we started out as being Africans. That's what they use to call us and that is what we used to call ourselves. Now I like the term "New Afrikan". But it doesn't make any difference as long as you know it when you are talking about yourself. If you don't know when you are talking about yourself, then you've got a problem. Malcolm used the term "African American", but he was very clear about why he used the term "African American". Malcolm said that just because you are a kitten born in the oven that don't make you a biscuit. He pointing out that we are Africans born in America. It is because of the culmination of history that we are a little bit of a lot of things, in truth. I like the term

"New Afrikan" because I think we really have to struggle against the immense imperialist power of the United States.

The question of self-determination is not just a question of establishing something of our own— that's an important part of it—but you have to understand that no two powers can occupy the same space at the same time. That's a fundamental principle of physics as applied to human dynamics. No two powers can occupy the same space at the same time. So if some power is occupying the space of your community, of your territory, of your energy, of your workplace, then in fact you cannot occupy that space at least as a parallel power, you become a junior power. You become an underling. Somebody that is controlled. So we have to some fighting in order to throw off the yolk of imperialism . When I say fighting I'm talking about in terms of our writing, in terms of our electoral strategy, in term of our economic development strategy. We have to understand that it's not just a question of allowing racism and repeated abuse of ourselves and others and understanding that these exist, but that these have to be undone. We have to be empathetic to other folks that suffer the same problems that we suffer in America. Although we suffer perhaps to a greater degree, we have the Mexicans, we have the Puerto Ricans, we have the people who are Indians of the various different respects, or the original Red Nations. Not only the ones that we identify as such, but the ones in Hawaii, the ones in Alaska that have become victims of the same thing. We have to understand that this a prison house, an empire, a prison house of nations, and all of these constructive energies of these nations for self-determination must be released so then we can come together on a voluntary basis and create that association of the Americas if that is what we want to do. And at the same time we must be very conscious of what must be done in Africa.

What we are doing in Mississippi is this. All around the country we face some serious challenges in terms of gentrification. Gentrification is one of the main weapons being used and the main anti-self-determination weapon around. I live in Jackson, Mississippi. I live in a county that is 75% black and a city that is 85% black. More importantly, it is important to understand that I live in what we have renamed—what we have taken opportunity to rename the western part of Mississippi—the Kush District. That's what we call it. So all the way from Oktibbeha which is in the north to Wilkinson county in the south, on the western part of Mississippi—those are 18 contiguous counties. Of those 18 counties 17 of them are solidly black. Three are the blackest counties in the United States. And one of the counties that is not predominantly black is Warren County where Vicksburg sits and 47% black and teeters between being predominantly black and predominately white. And what we do is work to elect someone to the council and eventually to the mayoralty. We are not just looking for a city, we are looking for a region of the country.

We have to understand that not only in terms of politics, but in terms of economics. We cannot have knuckleheads in office because we have to understand that you have to use the public sector in order to seize the ability to create wealth in the private sector. We have to create wealth for our people. We have to look at not only consumer cooperatives, but we have to look at producers' cooperatives. There are all kinds of businesses coming into Jackson and trying to develop and take over particularly the downtown area. Jackson has a double A ++ debt rate so that means that if the city borrows money companies will come in and try to get at the money and then develop their industries. It used to be that they would talk about ball parks, but now they are talking about hotels. They want everything. So they want to get that money. And they will promise you things, like: "We'll give you a few jobs." I don't want just a few jobs. I want to own the hotel. We want to own the hotel. We have to hold out and use this.

What makes what we are doing in Mississippi so important is that it's a region. What we are trying to do is take over the state. We want the whole state. We are 40% of the state. And it didn't take us with this gifted information about self-determination to come down and convince the people of Mississippi that they should elect their own people. Mississippi has more black elected officials than anywhere else in the entire country. You go through the Kush District, you got black sheriffs, you got black mayors, you got city council people; some of them are knuckleheads and some of them are not. But the reality is that the importance of our mission is to educate them about what is possible and educate about where we need to be headed.

What we are trying to do is convince you folks in Chicago that have run from Mississippi to come back home. We are trying to stabilize the population in Mississippi and to then introduce more blacks into Mississippi. Because we had an election just a little while ago for the governor, and the governor, the guy that won, was a white boy, a racists' republican, a reactionary republican. He's against immigration, he's against everything—if you are for it he is against it. So he won, but he won by 60% to 40%. 40% is the population of black people in the state. The fella that he beat was a black republican. So all we need is some more of y'all to come down. Atlanta had 500,000 black people immigrate to Atlanta in a 10 year period from the mid 80s to mid 90s. That was because of Mayor Jackson's insistence that the development at the airport would be inclusive of black ownership and black development and he insisted on that, even though they got ready to close down the whole airport project. White folks said we ain't going to even build it if he's going to keep on insisting like that. The mayor said it isn't even going to happen.

So when you walk through the Atlanta airport today and see all those black people around selling this that and the other...

What we need is to get a project which complements our international initiatives and I say that project be what we call the New Justice Frontier. We call it that because we all respect justice, because you know we lacked a lot of justice, but we fought against it and we are going to win, we are going to beat it. It's not just political, its economic, really economic, and it's also going to be social. And what we do very much embraces the works that we are doing here on the human rights agenda.

I am going to ask you to come down on September 13 when we will have a national justice conference. We want to explain to folks the aspects of this international movement that we are involved in.

JOHN W. BOYD, Jr. is a fourth-generation black farmer, businessman, and civil rights activist. As the founder and President of National Black Farmers Association (NBFA), he works to encourage the participation of small and disadvantaged farmers in gaining access to resources of state and federal programs administered by the United States Department of Agriculture. Boyd founded the NBFA after encountering the US Department of Agriculture's discriminatory practices first-hand and meeting many more black farmers who shared this experience. Boyd helped to bring the plight of black farmers to the nation's attention by leading NBFA members in a march on the White House, meeting with President Clinton, and to testifying before Congress. He has been featured in *The Washington Post,* "60 Minutes," "Nightline," CNN and as ABC News Tonight's "Person of the Week." He is a past nominee for the NAACP's highest honor, The Springarn Award, and currently ranks as one of *Ebony Magazine*'s most influential African Americans

THE LAND IS THE KEY

JOHN BOYD

It's a pleasure to be here this morning and to see old friends and new friends. And you know. in this struggle that we are in. you often see the same faces, don't you? That tells you a lot about where we are, where we need to be and the so-called movement.

My name is John Boyd, I'm the president and founder of the Black Farmers Association. We have 109,000 members in 42 states. Many are land owners, many are supporters, and many are descendents of persons who used to own land.

People, if we want any type of justice, any type of social, economic justice, people have got to involve the land. The land is the key. I listen to leaders all the time with great ideas that never include land. If you don't include land in any type of movement, in any type of structural movement for our people, we'd be lost. Land is the essence of everything. Every step I take, every footprint I make requires land. You have to walk on someone's land. We are the only group of people in this country that do not produce enough food to feed ourselves. Hispanics have overcome that option, Asian Americans, white folks—don't worry, they will produce enough food to feed themselves. They will do everything because they are not going to starve to death. For a group of people that can't feed themselves, that creates the inability to think. Ask our ancestors in Africa. I've travelled to many countries in Africa and they have some of the richest soil. I look at the soil content between African countries and the soil content in America, and I wonder why people are starving there. "Well," they say, "Dr. Boyd, if you went to bed hungry last night and you went to bed hungry the night before, you are not focusing on planting a seed, you are focusing on survival." That's a big difference isn't it? I can go out of here and eat whatever I want to eat today if I have some money in my pocket. But they can't do that in some of these countries. The plight of the black farmers is no different than the plight of black farmers in Africa. It's about the land.

This is the struggle in America, people, why we were brought to this country in the first place, in chains and shackles and in slave ships. We were brought to this country to work the land, to work the land for free. Many of us became great Agriculturalists. My grandfather, Thomas Boyd, was a great farmer. He was a great teacher. He was a great educator. As a matter of fact he gave me the knowledge and wisdom that I have today to move forward. As a little boy he told me that the land knows no color, it does not mistreat anyone. He said people do. He said you can go out and get the highest education, a Ph.D., but you cannot leave your Ph.D. to your children. I can leave my poor old raggedy farm to my children to carry on my name and legacy. These are things that we have forgotten as black people in this country. We want to, so called, run away from the land, and we moved up south, as I call it. Those from Mississippi came to Chicago. If you lived in the Carolinas you went to D.C. or New York City. You just drive straight ahead on 95 so you can get to the city because you want to leave what you thought wasn't your home. You wanted to leave what you thought was a bad situation. But I want to tell you that land ownership is the most powerful tool that you can possess. A person that owns land can go out and borrow money, can go out and do things, you can go out and build communities.

When I was listening to some of the conversations yesterday, about how people live in gated communities, how things happen to them. But when you live on your own farm, your own people were your neighbors, and they look out for you. It didn't matter what happened over on the weekend. You know, culturally what we do on the weekend, black people are still weekend people. They go out and drink whiskey and do things of this nature, but Monday morning it's back to work. Monday morning, I may need a cup of sugar while I am on the farm and I would say, Dr. Muhammad can I borrow a cup of sugar. He's going to say well you cussed me out yesterday, but go on in there and get that cup of sugar.

Because we have gone so far away from ourselves, culturally, you would say what Dr. Muhammad just said [grinning, "I ain't giving you no sugar"]. But because we needed one another then for survival, our communities were a lot better, our children were a lot better. Because

Dr. Muhammad you could beat my child if we lived on a farm and if that child does something wrong. And guess what, I wouldn't see anything wrong with that. But now if you say something to another person's child of that gated community, all of sudden you are the worst person in the world. People, we gotta get back to the basics. Land ownership, family structure. People, the key to success is your family. It's your family and having your children in the same house with you. Not having 4- or 5-baby mommas not taking care of your children. You are doomed from the start if you don't watch your children.

I'm going to let it all hang out. So when you play this tape, play it back from A to Z, don't edit it. Start at the beginning of the speech not the end, not at the middle. Don't edit my comments. Play the whole tape because people have a tendency to change things over the years and well this is what John Boyd said. That's not what I said. Play that whole tape.

People, the black farmers' movement was a pure movement. We didn't have all the people that we needed and all the support that we needed. We fought, we argued, we done everything. And I used a mule. Why did I use a mule? Because anybody over the age of 50 knows the importance of the mule to black people and black survival in this country. There are children that did not know. "What the hell is that man out there doing with a mule? That man must be crazy." No I'm not. I use a mule because we would be able to recognize it. "Oh, we have one of them on our farm too." What black person in this country with a farm did not have a mule? You didn't have a tractor, you had a mule. So I use the mule to symbolize our struggle.

Now the Department of Agriculture renamed it the Last Plantation, and rightfully so. The Last Plantation had a significant arm in taking away land in this country. At the turn of the century black people owned nearly 20 million acres of land. Today we are down to less than 3 million acres of land. Now the Department of Agriculture had an Accounting Committee that pretty much today consists of all white males that make the decisions on farm loans and farm ownership. And what they did after the Civil War, because the money had been spent and they said that black people were free to go, most of them had large families and needed to feed them. So where were they free to go? They wound up staying on these plantations and they ended up getting land down in the swampy areas and the hilly areas where the land was not productive. The same way that my grandfather received the land that his father left to him; it was way back in the woods and was hilly and it was not the best land. But people, land is land. And we have to make a decision, is our land ownership going to be for our survival the way it is in other countries? The Gaza Strip. How many of y'all are familiar with the Gaza Strip? Man, they fight over the Gaza Strip. That one little piece of land. They are willing to shed blood to keep their land. And when we have family land and there are 10-12 children there: "We want to sell the land as soon as daddy dies. " "I need some money." "I live in Chicago, I ain't ever going back to that raggedy farm." People, the farm carries your name from generation to generation. Hold on to the land. The land has your public identity in that community. That's the Jones' farm, that's the Harold's farm. That's the Boyd's farm. That's what we came from. That's what your daddy and forefathers worked for.

And then the newer generation that doesn't understand the significance of the civil rights movement, slavery. They say see it as an opportunity to buy a new car. "Buy me some new clothes." "I need to pay some bills." But if you do something structural with that land you can do anything with land. People, you'll have more than a new car. You'll have more than a new suit of clothes. Everybody seems to understand the importance of land ownership and really grasp the concept of land ownership except for our people.

Now I want to talk a little bit about what happened with the black farmers' movement. There were 3 bills that were passed into law early in the 90s when I first met James Byron. Me and James wrote the original lawsuit in my home. And we were debating about calling the National Black Farmers Association the National Black Farmers Association. That's self-determination. They said, no, call it the Minority Farms. That debate went on before the original board members that night. We were debating that, and my lights went out. They turned my lights out because my light bill was past due. And I said, there it is, the National Black Farmers Association.

Now people, we have filed that lawsuit in many states in the south: Georgia, Mississippi, Arkansas, Louisiana, Texas. That wasn't a new case, people, this case and the struggle has been going on for me for over 30 years. I first spoke about this case with Jimmy Carter to give you some idea, and every president since then I've spoken to about the plight of black farmers and land ownership and discrimination and what the black farmers have endured in not having the ability to receive loans.

And the other half of that fight that go lost in struggle with the United States Department of Agriculture was the banking system. Not just for black farmers, but for every black person, every black business owner in this country. If we do not get a grasp on this banking system and start raising concerns and issues about the dollars that are being lent, we're missing the boat. Every political person should be talking about access to credit. If you want your people to prosper, you need access to credit. If you want to expand your business, you need access to credit. If you want to be able to send your children to fine schools and colleges, you need access to credit. But that's not what we have today. We have a banking system dominated by four major banks. And people, their interest is not in lending you resources. So we also need to be concerned about the banking system.

Now we have had some wins and some, what I like to call, partial victories. Now, people say, well black farmers got an early settlement in the 90s, but many of the black farmers did not hear about the settlement. More than 80,000 black farmers came after the filing deadline. These farmers are what we call by definition, late filers. The first bill that passed—and Cynthia McKinney was involved in that bill—the statute of limitations bill that allowed the two year statute of limitations to be waived and those cases would be able to be heard going back to 1983 through the time span of December 31, 1996. So you have to have filed a complaint between those years. And the reason why they used those years is because the Civil Rights Office at the United States Department of Agriculture was closed under the Reagan Administration and there were thousands and thousands of complaints that were found at the Department of Agriculture with years of dust on them. Actually, we wanted the complaint to go back to the early 40s. The 40s is what I was petitioning for. And here again in the movement you often have to do things that you don't want to do. So we ended up 1981 through December 31, 1996.

And then there was the late filers bill. That was a bill that Cynthia McKinney spoke of briefly, the bill that reopened the lawsuit. That bill took a 10 year time period to get through both chambers of the House and Senate. That bill allowed the 80,000 black farmers to restate their claim in the settlement that passed into law in 2008. After that, when I thought we were over that hurdle—this is what they do, every time you think that you win they throw another stumbling block ahead of you. "Oh, the case is reopened because we do not have any money to compensate you all." So from 2008 to December 8, 2010, it took me another two years on the Hill.

And people, Capitol Hill, and Congresswoman McKinney can tell you, you will come in that door one person and you will leave that door another person. Because compromising to get something done for your people is what the bottom line was for me. Do I take a half of loaf and give some relief to 80,000 black farmers, many who have been in that system for so long waiting for justice, or do you wait it out with the possibility of getting nothing for the people? And the answer is real simple for me: a starving people can't fight. If you are starving you can't fight. If you're starving you can't lead your people. Every now and then you gotta have a victory so that you can move on to the next fight.

In the reparations movement—because the black famers, I don't know if you read the dictionary, but if you read the dictionary—an apology, land ownership, and money, people, that is what reparations is. This was a model that you can use in the reparations movement. But what happened? If you want to know the do's and don'ts, I can tell you what is going to work and what ain't going to work. But people, that's what it has to come down to for us, for our group of people. Do we do some things that can work or do we want 100% of everything that we want that we may never get?

It's about power. People, you gotta go out and take it. They ain't going to give you no power. They did not give us a settlement. We fought for that settlement tooth and nail. We were willing to fight and stand up on every corner 'till somebody heard us, with a mule or with a tractor in Washington, D.C., until somebody heard us. And if we want justice we gotta be willing to take it and do those kind of things that are not in the textbooks. What I learned in the textbooks was not what went down on Capitol Hill. It don't go down that way on Capitol Hill. What they teach you at these fine universities, you had better have the political power of persuasion. If you can't persuade 400 plus members of Congress and hundred members of Senate, at least the majority, that your position, that your needs and your wants and issues, warrant merit, then you probably going to get a few thousand.

Trayvon Martin isn't about right and wrong, it's about race. It's about race. And you listen to some of the commentators on Fox, well this said this and this said that. Two things happened there: Mr. Zimmerman is living and Trayvon Martin is dead. And they were in a tussle. People, that's what happened. Anything else in between, you can say whatever you want but the facts speak for themselves. And Trayvon Martin is pretty much an example of everything wrong in this country. And if we want to fix that system and if we want to make this reality better for our children, people, we gotta be willing to put it all on the line. If we want our lives to better for our children and the next generation, we gotta be willing to put it all on the line.

Where are our children today? This place should be full of young people. I make my children travel with me when I travel around. "Oh daddy I don't want to go." "Yeah, you going. You going." And that's what happened to our children, they've strayed so far that they cannot get back home, people. We gotta take some responsibility for the future of our children, and the future of our people. We are all leaders, we can start right in our own homes and take that and put it into effect.

But as I close today, I want to tell you, don't give up. I want to tell you that your dreams can become a reality if you don't give up. Giving up is the absolute easiest thing to do. Doing nothing is the absolute easiest thing to do. Just lie in bed and end up with bed sores. Nothing good will happen to you if you do nothing. But don't ever give up. If you don't have two nickels in your pocket, don't give up. When friends and family tell you can't defeat the United States Department of Agriculture, don't give up. Cynthia McKinney, when they tell you you cannot be the president of the United States, don't give up. Don't ever give up. Don't ever give up on your dreams. Don't ever give up on your rights. Don't ever give up on justice. Don't ever give up on trying to change the world and make it as better as possible a place to live in.

HENRY L. ENGLISH Serves as the President and CEO of the Black United Fund of Illinois, which works to create, support, and sustain African American social, economic, cultural, and educational institutions and to improve the quality of life for African Americans through reliance on self-help at the local community level. He is also the Chief Fiscal Officer of the PEOPLE Programme (Public Elected Officials and others for Policy Leadership and Exchange). The PEOPLE Programme brings about the international exchange of ideas between Europe, the United States, and Africa to help craft programs and policy innovations that identify ways in which residents of inner city communities can forge relationships with people from other nations to advance mutually beneficial programs and policies.

POLICY DRIVES AFRICAN AMERICAN CONDITIONS

HENRY L. ENGLISH

I want to cover a couple of areas. One will be what we do at the Black United Fund (BUF). Then, where are we right now as a as a people and where should we be going.

At BUF, we are 27 years old. We started with the notion that we would create an institution and that it would take 20 years to do that. We believe that we have achieved that. We are an institution and we are institutionalized. In other words, tomorrow if I have to take transition, we won't miss a beat—maybe one beat.

There are a couple of things that we do. One is that we work with community-based organizations (CBOs). And we do that in several kinds of ways: one, we provide financial assistance; two, we provide technical assistance, support services, and we also do raise money collectively on their behalf. We have slightly more independence than other organizations because we rely on individual donors in order to move the organization forward and satisfy our objectives. The third thing that we have kind of moved over into is training. There is a particular reason why we moved over into training, because we do not normally provide services to individuals. We work with organizations around building capacity so that they may grow and provide more effectively services to the communities that they serve. Building capacity is one of our greatest challenges. If we are talking about sustainability, if we are talking about independence, we have to talk about building capacity and how we get there. So that is what we concentrate on—building capacity of organizations and helping them to grow. Our job is to change people's lives. We look at ourselves and if we are not affecting individuals' lives, then we are not doing our job. If we look at our elected officials and they are not affecting the lives of those individuals that they represent, then they are not doing their job. And they should be held accountable. We elect them not only to represent us, but to also to change lives within the community that they serve.

So that is kind of a back drop of who we are and what we do.

Let's talk about where we are, now. We are an area community-based organization for the state but we're located in South Shore, so we decided that with our direct services we would just look at a microcosm of the African American community. And South Shore is that because it has mixed incomes and we have everybody living in there from the Minster to Reverend Jackson. We have the very well off to the very poor. We have everything that you would find in general society in terms of income, socio-economic status, all of that living in one community. So our job was to say: how can we affect change in this community to improve the quality of life of those individuals living there? We took on that challenge, and now we have been at it for about 3 years.

Now around a couple of issues: one, when we look at our community it is no difference then if I went to Mississippi. The same things happen here that happen in a small town in Mississippi. If I went to Detroit I would see the same thing. If I went to L.A. I would see the same thing. One thing that I see is high incarceration rates. We represent 13% of the population of the United States, but we have 42% of our people incarcerated. The United States has the highest incarceration rate of any country. Not just by a little bit, but by a big margin.

What else do I see? High unemployment rates. The unemployment rate among the 18-30 year olds within our community is about 60%. They have a lot of time on their hands.

What else do I see? High dropout rates. That's driven by the low quality education that our kids receive.

When we you put all of this stuff together it creates a great dilemma. I was just at a conference in Washington, D.C. last month that had research coming out from all over the world about inequality. Of course we wanted that conversation talking about inequality for the majority, basically the majority in this country and majority in European countries. Although the data was there, when we look at inequality we are in a double dilemma. This country has not experienced this type of inequality since the '30s. They found a balance in 1942. It started getting out of balance around 1975 and that balance has sky rocketed to the point where capitalism, not just in the United States but in the world, is in crisis right now. So we get a double whammy. Like I said at the conference, "You guys got a nose bleed, but we are hemorrhaging." So you are going to hear more and more people talking about inequality and plays and turn to talking about the 1%. And it has played itself out because capitalism is in a crisis and it has to come back into balance because there are dire consequences if it continues going in that direction. Where 25% have more than 50% of the wealth and 1% having 50% more than that. So it's out of balance. We are dealt with a double dilemma. Economically we are out of balance, and we get the brunt of it. And it plays itself out in these high numbers. But we get a double whammy. We have always experienced inequality. It has played itself out ever since we have been in this country from slavery to Jim Crow. It has played itself out to the point where we are right now.

I don't believe that we have been in this kind of crisis, this deep of a crisis before in our community. It is not going to stop. The Trayvon Martin case, to me, was about young black men being murdered in our communities and no one going to jail. I mean nobody goes to jail. Which means that there is no value for our young black people. There is no value for their lives. Then they become gangbangers. So being in the military during war, the first thing you do is make your enemy subhuman and it plays itself out, making it psychologically easier to blow their brains out. So now all our kids are gangbangers, dropouts and they are not important. So they can just kill each other and nothing is done about it. If you are a thief and you can go into that store and steal without anybody stopping you or trying to apprehend you, you can keep stealing. If there is no consequence for a kid shooting another kid, then they will keep doing it and then they will say that the reason they cannot solve it is because you cannot say who did it. But that is what we have police for, that is their job. And the victims now become the perpetrators. It's your fault that the kids are killing each other. There are probably a whole of things that are going on in our communities that are creating a situation where that happens, and you add no importance to it. I live in a community where sometimes I have to step over a body and a young man got shot on my block; he laid in the street for five hours uncovered. And when the coroner finally came they turned him over and let him lay there uncovered for another 2 hours. The Trayvon Martin case is about the fact that there is no value for young black life or black life period, so therefore there is no push to do anything about it. Yet when you look at the arrest records, they are still sending our kids to jail.

Where do we go from here? When we get back to land, we get back to ownership, we get back to control. And one of the things we started to look at when we took on this project is that we didn't start with glass being half empty, we started with: what do we have? What kind of assets do we have out here? When we start looking at those assets that as a community we had,t we discovered that as a community we have a lot more assets than deficits. But how will we use those assets? They are not being used to benefit the community. For example, one of the reasons we started the training program was because our young men were standing on the corner selling cigarettes or CDs and anything else they could sell, and at the same time they were watching people come into the community, because we buy a lot of goods and services on a day to day basis. These are basics things. There is nothing earth shattering about what I am saying. These are basic things that most communities control. We don't.

We got to a point where we decided, well, we got all these assets, let's redeploy these assets where it benefits people in this community. In other words, take control of the community economically. We already got control politically, but we need to take control economically.

Well how do we do that? So we decided we'll train the young people in how to provide these goods and services and train them to the point where they are competitive. In other words, where they are able to compete with anybody in terms of that service. And then encourage the community to hire them. We were going to convince the community to hire them. When we would send a young man out, a young lady out to do work, we got the response we wanted to get. Good customer service. Good quality of work. We have 100 more like that.

So we have to take control of the assets that we have and redeploy those assets. At the same time we do have human rights issues that we have to tackle. Fortunately we do have organizations such as this, that do tackle those issues and we should all be supportive. If we are going to control anything, we have to build capacity to do that. If you do not have the capacity—we have more elected official now then we have ever had but things have gotten worse.

This is nothing new. We talk about it all the time and frame it in different ways, but it boils down to this: that on a day to day basis when I drive to work, I see everyone working except for our young people. There is something wrong with that picture, which means that we are not effectively using our resources. So we have to make a decision as a group. And this was a country of groups since it was founded and I do not see that changing any time soon. The same people that came here still live together. And I did not see that changing. What needs to change is equal opportunity for everybody regardless of what group you come from.

What I am concerned about is equal access to opportunity. We train our kids. For example, the unions are not letting any of our people into apprenticeship programs. So what we said was well ok, if you won't accept our kids into apprenticeship programs we'll train them anyway and we'll create jobs for them and apprenticeship opportunities for them ourselves. And so when a job starts we will get more than a flag way job, we have carpenters and plumbers that are ready to move right in there for those jobs. We have enough assets in our community to do that.

I got up this morning and looked out and I did not see any white horse riding down the street to save us. So we have to do it ourselves. Any African American community that you look at has assets. I don't care how poor it is. We have to get back to supplying jobs to ourselves. If we are talking about self-determination, if we want to be self-determined you have to have the capacity for that and it starts right in your own community. Take that community and take control of that community. Train and educate the kids to take care of and make that community prosperous. And give them the skills necessary to maintain it. If we do not do that we will still be having this conversation 10 or 20 years from now. Nothing will change because we do not control the business or land. No one is going to give us control, we have to take it.

That is where we are and our world view of things. Now it's not earth shattering but if this took place across all of our communities you would see a change, a drastic change. And also with that change you would see a great amount of power come with it. You have to be able to control your own community. Don't allow yourselves, the victims, to be looked at as the perpetrators. We are the victims and let's not get confused at all. Point the fingers where they need to be pointed but at the same time take control of your block and even the next block, and the next thing you know we have the whole community.

And make sure that kids are being educated in your community. Everybody knows, its common knowledge, what happens when a kid drops out of school at third grade. That's common knowledge. We have been getting that for a long time and more people begin to understand that kids drop out at the third grade. Physically, they are still there, but it just takes a couple of more years for that to play out. Now where do the kids that drop out go? They used to feed the prison industrial complex. Eighty percent of them go to jail. Eighty percent! All the data you look at is going to point to that.

When did it get to the point where we can't teach a kid how to read between kindergarten to 5th grade? And now they say the kids can't read or count because the parents can't read or count or that the parents are teenagers or that the parents are this or that. But we pay teachers to teach our kids. When I think back to my parents. We lived on a farm and my parents went to school when they could go to school. My father made it through 4th grade. My mother, since she is female, she made it through the 8th grade. Most could not help me with my homework, but they did instill in me a strong work ethic, a strong value for education but they couldn't help me with my math problems. We relied on school teachers to teach me how to read and write. They could go through my ABCs but we relied on teachers to teach me how to read and write.

We often look at these things that are happening to us and we talk about inequality and the system—this inequality and system are across the world. *That does not happen by happenstance. That happens by policy.* Policy creates inequality. If policy creates inequality and we look at marginal populations, in this country, its black folks. What if I looked at black folks in England? And Turkish folks in Germany? All these things that I went through are happening to them. So if that is true, then there has to be a public policy hidden somewhere behind the scenes that is driving that inequality. At that level there must be policy that drives it. And just the same, in this country there is written and unwritten policy that drives our condition, our state. I mean it is not a coincidence that when I walk in and try to get a loan, I cannot get any money. If I try to get capital, I cannot get it. But the person that just got off the boat can go in and get a loan. So for these kind of things to happen in this concerted way, it has to be driven by public policy. I do not know where it's at, but I know it's there. We need to find out where it is and change it.

KAMM HOWARD operates apartment, retail, and office spaces on the south side of Chicago, Illinois. He is also a leading figure with the National Coalition of Blacks for Reparations in America (NCOBRA). He has served on the National Board and is currently the National Co-Chair of its Legislation Commission working to get HR 40, the Commission to Study Reparations Proposals for African Americans Act, passed into law. Kamm co-founded the Amos N. Wilson Book Club and the Amos N. Wilson Institute. The Institute operates as a Black think tank and means for propagating and testing the power theories of Dr. Amos N. Wilson. Kamm, along with Pat Hill, convened the 2011 International Year of People of African Descent Coalition for African Descendants of Chicago also know as IYPAD-Chicago, with the mission "to educated, mobilize, and organize people of African descent in Chicago around IYPAD banner to promote the right for self-determination

ECONOMICS OF SELF-DETERMINATION
THE AFRIKAN DESCENDANT NATION IN AMERICA

KAMM HOWARD
NCOBRA—CHICAGO CHAPTER[1] &
THE AMOS N. WILSON INSTITUTE

As early as 1852 some leading Afrikans in America have identified ourselves as a distinct people—a *nation-within-a-nation*, and have attempted to organize this population for self-determination. Martin Delaney was the best early proponent.

> Every people should be their originators of their own designs, the projector of their own schemes, and creators of their events that lead to their destiny—the consummation of their desires.
>
> Situated as we are, in the United States, many, and almost insurmountable obstacles present themselves. We are four-and-a-half million in numbers, free and bond, six hundred thousand free, and three-and-a-half million bond.
>
> We have native hearts and virtues, just as other nations; which in their pristine purity are noble, potent, and worthy of example. We are a nation within a nation as the Poles in Russia, the Hungarians in Austria, the Welsh, Irish and Scottish in the British dominions.

> But we have been by our oppressors, despoiled of our purity, and corrupted in our native characteristics, so that we have inherited their vices and but few of their virtues, leaving us in character, really a broken people....
>
> Being distinguished by complexion, we are still singled out—although having merged in the habits and customs of our oppressors—as a distinct nation of people. [Carruthers, 15.]

Since then, there have been many champions organizing and working toward that reality: Marcus Garvey with the Universal Negro Improvement Association and African Communities League; Elijah Muhammad with the Nation of Islam; El Hajj Malik Shabazz with the Organization of Afro-American Unity; Gaida and Omari Obadele with the Republic of New Afrika, and many meaningful others.

As such, and like any nation, the Afrikan-descendant nation today must be about the business of developing and organizing its own economy if it is to survive, satisfy its various needs, and allow for the full actualization of its potential.

> The idea that the Afrikan American community can exercise effective power, political or otherwise, without simultaneously exercising economic power is a fantasy... Neither will it measurably increase the probability of its future survival... and will remain relatively weak as long as it remains in relative [economic] disorder and will not amass and effectively utilize significant wealth." [Wilson, *Blue Print*, 349]

Economics can be defined as "the study [and/or practice] of the allocation of scarce resources to meet the infinite and competing wants of a people." Ayittey, 311. If the wants include, in addition to the satisfaction of material wants, sovereignty, self-reliance, autonomy, internal safety and security, self-actualization, i.e., *self-determination*, a society must factor these in when establishing and organizing its economy.

When we examine the economic configuration of the Afrikan descendant nation, we will see that none of the higher wants are even taken into consideration. To illustrate this, let's look at five economic characteristics of our community that stand out: 1) size and diversity, 2) wealth, 3) employment, 4) how its dollars circulate internally, and 5) its trade arrangements with other nationals within America.

1. Size and Diversity

Sometime in 2012, the Black economy in America is to reach $1.1Trillion. When this value is cited, usually the conversation is framed in two ways. The first is its size in relation to politically independent nation states. "If we were a nation, we would be the so-and-so largest country in the world." This is heard often. Continuing in this vein, in fact, the Black nation in America would be 16th largest, nearly on par with South Korea and Mexico and would be included in the G-20 (or 20 largest national economies). Conceptually this can be positive in putting it out there like this. It lets those who are organizing for self-determination compare its resources in the context of global economic strength (or weakness, if disorganized, as it now exists).

Secondly, the Black economy is framed as "spending power." No other economy is framed in this way. When other economies are discussed, their degree of diversity is a telling indication of their strength or weakness. For instance, according to the *CIA World Fact Book 2011*, both Mexico and South Korea have "modern" economies, organized for military defense, low and high-industrial production, space exploration, science and technology, agricultural production, finance, resource extraction, telecommunications, etc, in addition to manufacturing, distributing and ***consumption*** of consumer goods.

The Black economy, as it currently exists, is like many African mono-crop economies.

> Like many diasporan Afrikan nations and communities, Black America exports only one "cash crop" or commodity. That commodity is *labor*. And like many "dependent" Afrikan nations and communities, its sole export commodity is devalued by White America. More ominously, not only is its labor commodity being steadily discounted by White America, it is increasingly no longer being bought at any price. [Wilson, *Blue Print,* 385-386.]

So we see the Black economy has one primary source—wage labor—and is [un]organized primarily for consumption. So when the Black economy is framed only as "spending power," the Black community actually projects and prophesizes continued weakness.

2. Wealth

Per captita or family wealth is also considered when assessing the economy of a nation. Below are some facts about Black family composition and wealth.

- Median wealth of all families Black $5,577
- Median wealth of all Single Black Women of working age $1,000
- Median wealth of all Single Women age 36-49 $5,000
- 32% of 2 parent families Median net worth of $31,500

In some of these areas, it is many times greater for whites. For instance the median wealth for white families is $113,149 (20 times higher) and for single white women of prime working age is $46,500 (nearly 10,000 times that of Black women)

- 72% Children live in Female headed households
- 43% Female-Headed Families are living in "poverty"
- 39% Children, approx 7 million, living in "poverty"
- 27% or 11,345,000 Blacks live in "poverty

The last statistic is similar to that of developing countries and not that far from those that are maldeveloped, (nations pejoratively called "third world countries.") Presently Ghana has a similar impoverishment rate.

3. Employment

Nationally in the U.S., as of May 2012, the *unemploy-men*t rate was 8.2%. It is more than double that for Blacks in America at 16.9%. Focusing on Black males, it is nearly three times the national rate, at 21.2%. This, however, is not a real indicator of the employment picture for Black men. A better indicator is labor force participation or the actual employment rate. The Black male labor force participation rate in the 40 largest Black population centers in America is 49.9% for men ages 16-64. However when we break it down for young men ages 16-24 it is at 27%. And for those young men 16-20. It is less than 10%,. That is, **nine out of ten of these young men do not have work.**

When we look at the Black family, Black male labor force participation (BMLFP) has been the *key indicator* of the health, wealth and stability of that unit. In fact, it has been the single correlation factor that "determined" the level of two-parent family composition since 1865. In the Illinois Trans Atlantic Slave Trade Report, Prof Linwood Talheed looked at labor participation vis a vis two parent family composition and found that their rates moved in tandem, with father present homes maintaining 12-18 points below that of labor force participation. Whereas from 1870-1920 BMLFP averaged 94%, during that same period 2 parent families averaged 77%. From 1930 to roughly 1965 there as a steady decline in BMLFP with father presence declining to 69% Then, beginning in 1965 with the exporting of manufacturing jobs, continued racial prejudices and power differentials, the exclusion from unions, deskilling etc, the Black male begin to be precipitously excluded from the workforce, and like the previous hundred years, we had a concomitant decline in two-parent families at nearly identical rates. Year 2000 BMLFP rate was 68% and the two parent family rate was 41%, holding identical to the spread first noted in 1870. So in 2012 where there is less than 50% male labor force participation across the board, and with marriageable-age males considerably lower, we have less than 38% of families of the two-parent type.

4. Dollar Circulation

Moving to the internal circulation of the resources within the Black community, this too is an indicator of the poor organization of the tremendous economic resources of this community.

Nationally, with a population 42,021,000, the Black community boasts 1.9 million businesses. This is a very respectable 1:22 business to population ratio. Incidentally, according to the US Census, this is a 60.5% increase from 2002-2010, and was the fastest growing segment of US economy. A poor statistic, however, is that 94.4% of these businesses have no employees. This other 5.6%, or 106,824 businesses, employ 921,032 employees (avg. 8.6).

Combined, these nearly 2 million businesses grossed $137.5 Billion in receipts. This is roughly 12.5 % of $1.1 Trillion (up 55% during the same 2002-2010 period, also respectable).

In Chicago, one of the largest Black population centers with 992,000 Blacks, 58,632 Black-owned business operate (a 1:17 population to business ratio, better than the Black national average and better than that of the city's other ethnic groups—Arabs 1:37, Asians, 1:20). Chicago has the 2nd largest Black business base, New York is number 1; and Cook County (Chicago) leads the nation with 83,733 Black businesses in a county.

However, like the national Black business base, the Chicago employment picture is equally shallow. Ninety percent of Chicago's Black businesses don't have any employees. These businesses receive $6.8 Billion in receipts from a total city-wide Black economy of $41 Billion. This is 17% of the total annual economy. Better than the national average but well below that of what's needed to be spent to begin to empower the community. A full 83% of the income coming in is spent outside the community. The effect of this will be shown below.

5. Trade

The trade position of the Afrikan Descendant Nation can be said to be akin to its existing in a multinational trade war where we are the targets (victims) of all the other nations.

Blacks are operating fewer and fewer business in their communities that provide the basic needs and wants of this community. Foreign nationals and newly immigrant peoples have targeted this community for their wealth production, while bringing or fostering nothing of value back into these communities.

In the city of Chicago, this ethnic economic warfare can be shown by the following realities:

Arab nationals and immigrant Americans

- 185,000 in Chicago own over 5000 businesses 1:37
- 3-5 Families finance most of the stores
- Dominate Grocery operations in Black communities
- 1500 liquor stores
- Dominate non-chain fast food establishments
- Reported on the street to be selling guns and drugs out of some of these stores
- Blacks are locked out of their market (Arab-towns)

Korean nationals and immigrant Americans

- 59,000 own 3,000 business in Chicago 1:20
- Had a strategy to take over the Black beauty industry.
- Planned it in early 1980's
- Exist as a racial monopoly in the Black beauty industry, even locking Blacks out of an industry they created dating back to the late 1600's
- Control 80% of $6 Billion Black hair care industry nation-wide
- Also dominate in the apparel stores in Black community
- Owns the Nail business in the Black community
- Employ a few Black women in beauty supply and a few Black men for security in apparel operations
- Before being demolished, Koreans owned 72 business at the Englewood Mall in the heart of the inner city (roughly a three block strip)
- Locked out of their market—they own 70% Business in Korea-town.

Hispanic/Latino/South American nationals and immigrant Americans

- Act as the low cost leaders, engage in severe price

warfare
- Displaced the Black skilled and semi-skilled construction trade workers
- Established a thriving Lawn Care industry in the Black community
- Specialize in T- Shirts outlets
- Growing visibility in street cart sales
- Locked out of their markets

Indian/Hindu nationals and immigrant Americans
- Own the majority of Subway franchises in the Black community
- Own the majority of Motels in the Black community
- Share gas station market with Arabs
- 1% of Population
- Very limited employment of Blacks
- Locked out of their market

Chinese nationals and immigrant Americans
- Primarily provide ethnic cuisine
- On the surface this adds to diversity of food choice
- However, they employ 0% Afrikans
- Encroaching on the ownership of multi-family housing in the Black community
- Locked out of their market

Jewish subgroup and immigrant Americans
- Nationally dominate and control the 100,000's of jobs we created but don't fill in the sports and entertainment industry
- Uses their control over these industries to:
    - Foster racial self-hatred among Blacks
    - Create and nurture negative, self-destructive and stereotypical images of Blacks
    - depoliticize masses of Blacks
    - carry messages that decrease racial awareness

Anglo Saxon and Irish subgroups and immigrant Americans
- Dominates 2.4 million jobs within the $208 Billion national prison industry in the following areas
    - Judges
    - Prosecutors
    - Jailers
    - Investigators
    - Police
    - Clerks
    - Medical Personal

- Pharmaceuticals
- Psychologists
- Social Workers
- Post Incarceration
- Food services

Special note. Where it is indicated that Blacks are locked out of the immigrant markets, this means not only can we not operate in their communities, but they spend almost none of their resources with Black businesses. These two characteristics are the norm for all of the above groups —massive amounts of resources taken out, nearly zero resources put back in. This can not be considered trade, but an economic strategy consistent with warfare, hegemony, colonization and destruction. Dr. Wilson indicates the degree of destruction this arrangement foments and proscribes the only logical course of action:

> The denuding of inner-city communities of their resources and wealth... serve to **concentrate** poverty, joblessness welfare dependency, single-parenthood, teenage pregnancy, drug abuse, disease and sickness, poor education, crime – a complex interlocking set of social and economic disorders... Without malice towards [these groups], we must acknowledge that the tremendous outflow of [the varied] resources... at the hands of these agents ... cannot but grievously harm these communities...maintain and hasten ... the decline, ...accentuate and accelerate the ... social disorganization...[and] increase social problems.
>
> [The] community **must confront the fact**... it cannot continue to permit its vital resources to be commandeered by aliens. It **must aggressively accumulate external earnings, retain as much of its internal resources as possible and invest in itself first,** if it is to survive and prosper ... [*Blueprint,* pgs 349, 350.]

The purpose of this aggressive action—survival and prosperity—must achieve with it the following ten goals. It must:

- Shape New Economic Values
- Create Wealth Opportunities
- Amass Power
- Promote Full Employment

- Alleviate Poverty
- Increase Skill Base
- Enhance Internal Technology
- End Foreign Monopolies
- Determine and Direct Productive Output
- Control Politics and Create Policy

To address the Afrikan descendant economic structure in a way that re-orders it for the purpose of self-determination, the Amos N. Wilson Institute offers the following five suggestions:

1. Engage in Black Power Buying Behavior—spend more Black dollars with Black businesses with a purposeful decrease in the amount of Black dollars spent outside of the Black business community. Buy from Blacks when, where and what you can, and if you can't, don't buy. Use that money for investment in suggestion 5 below. Many campaigns have been aimed at this strategy—Double Duty Dollar (1940's and 50"s), Black Fridays (NCOBRA 1990's), and in Chicago, Dr. Web Evans's Buy Black campaign (1960's–present), Maggie and John Anderson's Empowerment Experiment. (2009- present) and the Triple Duty Dollar Campaign (upcoming, Amos N. Wilson Institute).

2. Capitalize on our consumption—the dominant form of Black economic behavior for the greater part of the 20th century, and continuing now, is consumerism. We must purposely go after the Black consumer dollar. This means bettering our current businesses to compete with others and creating new businesses to compete for the Black dollar. Secondarily, we must then begin to target for distribution and production many of these same consumption products.

3. Increase Employee Base—with the present numbers of Black businesses, the Black business communities could make a significant reduction in the unemployment numbers by expanding these businesses to take on employees. If each of the 1.8 million business that currently have no employees, added on average 3 employees, we would nearly employ all those willing and able to work who are now locked out of work. This should be a national agenda. *As, importantly, we must purposefully expand legal and licit opportunities in the informal economy.* The Amos N. Wilson Institute is taking the lead on this with the creation of the Kemet Communities League—the economic arm of the Institutive.

4. Engage in True Nationalism—In all things, Blacks must engage in activities that foster the building of a strong ethnic community. As power

in America is welded by ethnic communities, the Black community is the only community encouraged to act as individuals. (Wilson, Anderson) This community must seek to organize its economy and other institutions around the idea of internal interdependence and self-determination, whether internal or external.

5. Establish local, regional and national community investment funds—to engage in the aggressive action and achieve the goals stated above, the re-channeling (away from consumption) and the pooling of resources is a must... As Dr. Wilson admonishes us, "The Afrikan American community must create its own stable and productive investment infrastructure," (Blue Print, 396) this is how the Kemet Community League—the economic arm of the Amos N Wilson Institute—will begin the transfer ownership of the economic activity of this community to the community residents.

Only then will we be able to fully carry out all of our mandates given us by Dr. Wilson.

Finally, we leave these encouraging words—the Amos N. Wilson Institute's Creed:

> I love the challenge of being Afrikan in today's world. It's wonderful. I love digging in my heels against the impossible odds of being black in America! What greater challenge could we have in life today than to be Afrikan? What greater testament to our heroism than to overcome the problems that face us today? What greater opportunity can we have to transform ourselves and transform the world in the process? Why would we wish to escape this kind of challenge? It's too wonderful, too magnificent. We should eat this kind of challenge for breakfast!" (*Falsification*, pg 40-41)

REFERENCES:

Anderson, Claude. 2001. *PowerNomics: the National Plan to Empower Black America.* PowerNomics Corporation of America, Inc. Bethesda.

Ayittey, George B. 2006. *Indigenous African Institutions.* Transnational Publishers, Inc., Audley, NY.

Carruthers, Jacob. 1994. *African or American, a Question of Intellectual Allegiance*. Kemetic Institute, Chicago.

Levine, Marc V. 2012. *Race and Male Employment in the Wake of the Great Recession: Black Male Employment Rates in Milwaukee And the*

Nation's Largest Metro Areas 2010. University of Wisconsin-Milwaukee Center for Economic Development. Milwaukee.

Tauheed, Linwood. 2008. "A Secular, National and Regional Analysis of the Impact of Labor Market Discrimination on African American Socio-Economic Development (1870-2000). Illlionis Trans Atlantic Slave Trade Commission. Jacob H. Carruthers Center for Inner City Studies Northeastern Illinois University. Chicago.

Wilson, Amos. N. 1998. *Blue Print For Black Power. The Political, Economic, and Moral Imperative for the 21st Century*. Afrikan Info Systems. Trenton.

Wilson, Amos. N. 1993. *Falsification of Afrikan Consciousness. Afrikan Info Systems.* Trenton.

U.S. 2010 Census Bureau

ENDNOTES

1 The National Coalition of Blacks for Reparations in America.

PANEL FOUR

USING THE UN TO ADVANCE AFRICAN AMERICAN CONCERNS

- Why should African Americans bother with the United Nations?
- What means do African Americans have of participating in international diplomacy at the UN? At other governmental bodies?
- What are the advantages of engaging in international diplomacy?
- What are the various UN bodies through which the grievances and complaints of African Americans might be registered and addressed?
- What is Human Rights Monitoring and how can violations be addressed on the international level?

Left to right: Speakers Queen Quet, Atty. Standish Willis, and moderator Atty. Gregory Mitchell.

STANDISH WILLIS practices law in Chicago, Illinois, specializing in personal injury, criminal defense, and federal rights cases. Stan earned a baccalaureate and masters degree from The University of Chicago and later studied graduate economics at the University of Illinois-Chicago and earned a Jurist Doctorate from The Illinois Institute of Technology's Chicago Kent College of Law. During his over 25 years of legal practice, Stan advocated for the human rights of African Americans in US. courts and before international bodies including the United Nations' Committee to Eliminate Racial Discrimination (CERD); the Organization of American States' Inter-American Commission on Human Rights; and submitted reports as part of its Universal Periodic Review (UPR) of the United States. He also co-founded and co-chaired Black People Against Police Torture "BPAPT", a grass-root, community-based organization to insure justice in the Chicago police torture cases, and to build a Human Rights movement within the African American community. He also helped draft and successfully lobby for a bill titled "The Illinois Torture Inquiry and Relief Commission Bill" to create the Torture Commission, that would have the authority to review the cases of those 24 torture victims who remain in prison.

USING THE UN TO PUT PRESSURE ON AMERICA

STANDISH WILLIS

We are not under the illusion that the human rights mechanisms will solve all our problems in Chicago. At least I am not under the illusion and I am trying to make sure that my community is not under that illusion. It is another step forward for sure. When I am talking to audiences I remind them, particularly audiences from my community, that we have a history that goes back two decades of trying to advance our struggle into the human rights arena. The NAACP attempted in the 40s and of course there was the filing of the charge of genocide in 1951. We know that during the 60s a number of groups tried to raise issues before the U.N, SNCC (Student Non-Violent Coordinating Committee) and others. We know that Malcolm talked about, in Malcolm's words, "taking our case to the world court." So we have tried to do that. And there has been pushback on our doing that. Particularly we see some people did not want the Negro question going before a world body. And they pushed back to the extent that we were left with advancing our interests through civil rights only. And that has been a problem because civil rights does not have the remedies broad enough to address our problems. So I think this is the time.

I was telling my Brother Chokwe that I've been speaking a lot, more than I should be as lawyer who has an office, who has clients. I think during the first three months of this year, I've been to St. Louis Law School, I spoke at Loyola and DePaul all on human rights. I was down in Champaign. So people are interested. I am doing it because there is a need there. But I would like more people to step up so I do not have to do as many, because I have a law office that I have to run. I had a very interesting dialogue concerning human rights; I moderated a group of diplomats a few weeks ago from South America and the Caribbean. It was the "EBOLA" group. This is a group of South American and Caribbean countries that decided to pull together in a treaty formation to advance their countries and in some ways isolate the United States So after the diplomats from Venezuela, Bolivia, and from the Caribbean spoke, we met at Loyola Law School and it was very interesting. They would not let the Cuban diplomat come, so the Cuban diplomat sent a statement that was read by a Cuban professor. It was pretty interesting. So things are moving to human rights and the peoples' need to advance the right of self-determination.

We saw it brewing in the 60s and the 70s, and now we see it going different ways. It's very encouraging but requires a lot of work from the ground. And it won't happen in Geneva, although Geneva is part of it. And I'll indicate to you some of the history about how we try to keep communities involved. I organized a group called Black People Against Police Torture. Some of them are here. I recognized at the court addressing the first torture case, that although all the victims were African Americans, there weren't many African Americans at the table advancing the struggle and I know my people are interested in the issue. What was needed was an organized forum for black people to advance it. And no other civil rights organization was willing to provide the organizational structure needed to advance that struggle.

Black People Against Torture provided that organizational structure. We pulled together many community people and did a lot of various advanced things. We were first to take the position against the Olympics coming to Chicago based on human rights grounds. We invited John Carlos—some of you may remember John Carlos, the Olympian. We were first to raise the issue of reparations for the torture victims and I'll touch on that in a bit. I went to Geneva, Switzerland in 2008. The group insisted that I go. We took the position on judges that are involved in the torture cases. People don't go after judges enough. We did.

And we've done a number of things that grew out of that group for people that had ideas but did not have a forum to express those ideas. So when I went to Geneva in 2008, the first thing I did when I got back was to call a town hall meeting and report back to the community to get input from the community so that we could go forward. And that's critical because, I suggest that in relation to the United Nations and other international forums or the court, we have to build a people-centered movement on the ground, otherwise it would be meaningless and that is what we are trying to do.

So the police commander John Burge cases involved everybody. If you have a significant black population you have a significant amount of police violence. So in Chicago we watched the criminalization of black youth emerge and we fought it. We saw that when the police decided to attack the housing project, they call it a housing sweep. They would literally go and make everyone come out of the housing project and search the housing project and knock around some people because they said they were trying to combat gang and drugs. "Gang and drugs" became a code for black youth. We knew that so we challenged them. That was part of the criminalization. We saw our city council pass a law—an anti-lawyering bill—which gave police the authority to arrest anyone who was in the public way who did not leave the public way when the police ordered them to leave. They could be arrested. We challenged it in the city council. We came to some of our black alderman but they voted for it and they passed it. And every court in the circuit all the way up to the Supreme Court said that it was unconstitutional. So we had to reflect on why they passed it. They have real lawyers at the Cooperation Council that had obviously studied this bill but they passed it anyway. And I had to conclude that they were trying to design, they were trying to create a culture in the community where when black people, particularly youth, see police, they automatically disperse or they automatically walk over to the wall. Or they run. Even if the police don't say it, they feel that police are going to put something on them, take them in and hold them overnight, or something else that they should not be doing.

We saw the state legislative body passing laws—the mandatory minimum laws—all around the notion that crack cocaine was flooding the communities. And in fact crack cocaine was not flooding the communities any more than it was flooding the suburban white communities. But they were targeting our communities. We saw, for example, the Village of Riverdale had a law that says that you cannot wear gang-related clothing. In fact, during the late 90s if you went into a police station, you would see like a trophy case of jackets that they had taken from our children because they were "gang-related". The Village of Harvey, the school district, passed an administrative mandate that you could not wear gang-related hairstyles. And if you did you could be suspended from school. What were gang-related hairstyles? Braids, dreads, jerry curls etc. They were targeting our kids based on noncriminal conduct, noncriminal clothing, noncriminal hairstyles. And this was going on all over the country. So now we see our kids piled up in the principal's office. In Illinois we have more kids in prison than we have in colleges. That's a scary scenario for our future. So that's what's going on all over.

But we aren't even talking about that. We are talking about something that I have never seen before. And I don't think that wherever you came from you have ever seen anything quite like this. And we discovered it at my law office. I was at People's Law Office, when a young man asked us to represent him because he had been tortured, along with his brother Andrew and Jackie Wilson. Some of you may remember the shootout where these two brothers killed two police officers. And if you are from Chicago you will remember the reaction of the police to our community. They came through the communities like everybody was a criminal, putting guns to the heads of children and putting guns in the faces of older people until they found the persons who committed the crime. And they tortured Andrew Wilson. They tortured him by putting plastic bags over his head, like garbage bags, until he suffocated. They had what they called a "Nigger Box". This was an electric contraption that had a battery, sort of like what they used in the military in the old days when you are out in the fields and need to communicate. So you had these kinds of batteries and they would have a cable and prong and they would clip the clip on your earlobe or on your testicle or any other part of your body. And they would crank the electricity into your body until you confessed to a crime you did not commit. And they had a cattle prong. This is an electrical device used for cattle. But they use if for black men and black boys. They would take this devise and hit them on the skin or any part of their body until they caused them to break down and confess to these crimes. These heinous crimes. That got most of them life and several of them were on death row. Several of them, Marcus Wiggins, Bart Clemmings and others, were 14 or 15 years of age when these crimes were committed.

The more telling thing about it is that everybody knew about it. We didn't know about it. We learned about it in probably '88-89 when we got the call and decided to represent Andrew Wilson. When we went to trial in the case we started getting anonymous calls from police saying, "You haven't seen anything yet. This is the tip of the iceberg." We started getting letters from all over the state from prisoners, "That happened to me." And so when you think about it, these young black men are going before judges with their cases. Many of them if not most of them are filing motions because their statements were coerced, a motion to suppress. Judges are hearing the motions put before them, over and over, and they are saying in the motions that "They put a plastic bag over my head, they had this electrical device." It was out of area 2 on the south side of Chicago. The same detectives' names were coming up each time. No judge—none—stopped and said, "What the hell is going on here?" We think more than 200 instances. Nobody stopped it.

We learned later that not only did the judges have to know about it but many of the prosecutors that were involved had to go to the station and take the statements after the police had coerced the statement. This is called a felony review in order to bring formal charges. None of them said anything about it. And then we learned later that the state's attorney had been put on notice that this had happened. But when Andrew Wilson was tortured, the doctor sent a letter to the police superintendent and he sent it on to the state's attorney. The state's attorney was our former mayor, Mayor Daley. He did nothing about it. Had he said, "Wait a minute, I don't like what I'm seeing here, we are going to have an investigation", we predict that would have saved at least 70 victims from torture. But he did nothing about it. And still hasn't done anything about it.

We find out later that the County Board President at the time knew about it. He sent a letter to the doctor telling him to just kind of cool it. Don't spread this. So everybody knew about it. These cops did this with impunity, starting as early as the early 70s for at least 2 decades. So we finally built a movement around this and we went after them. John Burge got fired in the early 90s. They continue to provide his pension which is absurd given that he is in prison.

And so in 2005, by 2005, we had done just about everything one can do in a democratic society to get justice for these brothers. They were on death row at the time. Twelve of them would have been executed. We managed to get a special prosecutor named which was always a goal. We had demonstrations, all kinds of press quotes, and a hearing before the City Council for the Cook County Board and everybody else. We went to the U.S. Attorney's office, went to the Justice Department, and we went to the State's Attorney. You name it, we did it. The only thing we did not do was something that is not a part of the democratic society, even though we were tempted to do it.

So we were at an impasse. We were waiting for the special prosecutor —after "investigating" this for 4 and half years—to make his report. Well I came up with the idea, or I didn't really come up with the idea, I was home listening to Public Radio and they were airing a discussion about how Bush was trying to circumvent the Convention Against Torture and I guess the ancestors talked with me, what Malcolm said and others, and I said, wait a minute we are tortured here, why aren't we taking this to the international level? And so I convinced my colleagues that we should.

The first forum we turned to was the Organization of American States, the Inter-American Commission on Human Rights. And we decided to take it there because they have this general interest petition that you can file, and it's not as weighty as the U.N., but you could do it any time of the year. The treaties have periodic requirements. For example, for most of them the United States has its review every 4 years. With the Inter-American Commission you can file at any time. And the more important thing for us, if we got a hearing, was that it would be in Washington, DC. We figured we could afford to go to Washington, DC. If you get a hearing with the U.N. you have to go to Geneva, Switzerland. That's a whole different ball game. So we thought we could take a busload of folks with us. They gave us a hearing and we went and we put out our evidence. And I tell you it was a new experience. It was new, I had to search around and find out how to do all this because I've always felt that I was a human rights advocate but I had never done human rights as such. And so there were people that I had to reach out to. There was still a learning curve. It's new. I'm a civil rights lawyer. I've sued more police than you can count. I've sued probably every municipality in Cook County more than once. But the human rights I am learning provides remedies that I think we should advance.

So we filed it, and one of my colleagues went before the Committee Against Torture in 2005, 2006 and the Committee Against Torture—and this is the important part— made a finding and in their finding they talk about "areas 2 and 3 of Chicago police department" and they directed United States "to promptly and thoroughly and impartially investigate all of the allegations of act of torture or cruel, inhumane, and degrading treatment or punishment by law enforcement personnel and bring perpetrators to justice in order to fulfill its obligations under Article 12 of the convention. State party shall also provide information of an ongoing investigation."

This was in May of 2006. So last year, the same Committee, because there is another reporting requirement every four years—the United States by the way is always late. Well they are late because they are arrogant. They weren't complying at all until a few years ago. Now that American citizens are getting more involved they are slowly doing the reports that are required by the treaties. I think the more American citizens get involved in the future I think we can make our government comply, which can be very important. In 2010, this same body provided the United States with what is called a list of issues prior to the submission of the 5th periodic report. In other words: before you do your next report, this is what we want you tell us, based on your last report. And so they have in here, paragraph 25, "As requested by the Committee in its previous concluded observations, please provide updated information on the investigations and prosecutions related to the allegations of torture in areas 2 and 3 of Chicago police department. In this report please provide detailed information on the charges filed against John Burge and the outcome of this case. Furthermore indicate any other police officers who have been brought to justice in the case."

So when the United States files this report—we do not when it will be—they will have to again address this. So it's a level of accountability, but it's only a level of accountability if we are actively involved because the United States really doesn't care about the United Nations. But if we are pressing on this thing, then there becomes a level of accountability. And so we will be preparing, of course, the same way we did in 2005, to send our reports to the United Nations. Telling the United Nations Committee Against Torture what has really been happening because the United States will lie about it. They'll say "Oh we finally prosecuted Burge and everything's fine." But it's not fine. You prosecuted him. And I am convinced that it is the work that we did in bringing this to the international forum that caused the Justice Department to call the U.S. Attorney's office in Chicago to tell them to take this seriously. Because it was a matter of months before John Burge was finally indicted. So it was successful.

Now in our next report, I and others will be working on telling the United Nations that officers and many detectives have not been indicted, but also telling them that United States, Chicago Illinois, should provide reparations for these crimes against humanity to the tortured victims and the torture victims' families. Reparations is broad enough to include torture victims' families. Because when you send a young man off to prison, if he is 14, it's not just him who suffers, his mother suffers, his dad suffers, his siblings suffer. If he has children, his children suffer and the wife suffers. And just as important as reparations, is that the community suffered. Our community suffered because of what these police did. We suffer one way, we don't trust police. We didn't trust them much in the first place, but really don't trust them now. We have a long history of having no reason to trust them. They haven't done very much to gain our trust. So this is the mechanism that we think bought John Burge before the court.

Since that time last year, as you may know, there is a universal periodic report, the first one that the United States had to get involved in. It's a new mechanism organized by the United Nations. All countries have to be reviewed every four years regardless of the treaties. And many reports were filed. I filed one with another sister interested in this issue, I filed one raising the political prisoner related COINTELPRO[1] raising an issue that for me has long been unresolved. We have brothers in prison that have been there for 30 years. I thought this was the perfect forum to raise that issue. So we filed it. We got some play on it. With this Universal Periodic Review, unlike the CERD [Convention on the Elimination of All Forms of Racial Discrimination] or CAT [Convention Against Torture], the Universal Periodic Review is done by states reviewing other states. So we had to reach out to other states to get them to raise our issues related to the United States. We obviously had a limited number of states that we could reach out to. But the Cubans raised it, the Venezuelans raised it, and we tried to get others to raise it. And I think in the future we will get more support.

So those are the two filings. While we haven't had much movement on this, but I think that the embarrassment of the United States government does care. People say, "Why the U.N.?: The United States does not care about the U.N., but it does care about its role in the world community. When you are the biggest imperialist power, when you have over 100 military installations around the world, when you are, as Dr. King said, the greatest purveyor of violence, you can't not care. Because you cannot go into Iraq telling them what kind of government they should have when your citizens are saying that you discriminate against citizens in this country. It's a contradiction. So they care. And I think that's why John Burge is doing time. He's not doing enough time; he only got 4 years because we could not get him on torture because of the statute of limitations, thanks to the special prosecutor. But, and this is the reason I can tell you that there is connection between what we did, we actually met with the U.S. Attorney that was in charge of the Burge prosecution because they didn't have a clue. I'm in federal court 90% of time, and we were invited over to talk to them about the Burge case. And we explained to them how they could prosecute Burge. If you lie on federal interrogatories or if you lie in federal depositions, and it's within the 5 year statute of limitations, you can be prosecuted for lying. That's what they went after him on. They did not get it, but we had not only studied the law, but we had a chart of every lie and the year that it was said.

I will not take up any more time with this except to say, as I indicated, that there are a number of processes that we have used. I think that this is a good model for us. We struggled over two decades. It's a model because we saw communities organizing together around this issue. It's a model because I had the presence of mind, because of my history, to organize my community because I knew it was necessary. And black people being in the mix at that level made a big difference. So that's a model. It's a model because as progressives we don't like to be bothered by the legislative process too much. So we did this time. We lobbied for the Illinois Torture Inquiry and Relief Bill, which is now an Act. And that sets up a commission to review all of the torture victims that are still in prison. It's a law that has teeth. That has subpoena power. It's a commission. The only problem is that they began to cut the money back. So we fight to get the money. And they can recommend that these torture victims be released and get a new trial even though they have exhausted all of their other remedies. That's the critical thing. Most of these brothers do not have a remedy. The only way they would have a remedy is if there is newly discovered evidence, which is very rare. So we've done the post-conviction appeals, the habeas corpus, we've done everything. No more remedies, you die in prison, except for this Commission.

So in concluding, we need to build a people-centered movement around human rights. We cannot build that, and do not leave here with the illusion that I'm saying that whatever you are doing now you have to stop doing that and build this, because it doesn't work like that. Whatever you are doing now, you have to keep doing it. So you do more work. Sorry about that. It's the way it is in the movement. So it means we have to incorporate this. This is critically important for us. I've had this discussion with Kamm [Howard of N'Cobra] in terms of the reparations movement. We felt that we would have more success with reparations for African Americans if we were trying to do it in an environment where people understood human rights. We don't deal with human rights. Our remedies are civil rights remedies. Reparations is not a civil rights remedy. So if we create a climate of human rights, then reparations would resonate right away. That's what we are asking for, for the torture victims. It's much broader, much deeper and puts a burden on the government much more. So that's two things.

We have to build a movement and we cannot stop what we are doing. And it has to be a people-centered movement. We have to get beyond the charismatic leadership who will not work with the human rights movement. We cannot rely on "whoever" to come. We can't say, "When's Jesse coming?" Well we love Jesse, but he won't work with human rights movements. It has to be people-centered.

This government has a requirement under the three treaties it has signed to educate its citizens on human rights. Have you all been educated on human rights? Did you get it in public school? I didn't get it and I went to public school. But they have that requirement. So what happens is that we have a responsibility to try and educate our people and our community—which is what our government should be doing. The state should be mandating public human rights education. No question about it. There is no debate about that. But they don't. Why? *Because they don't want us to know.* You should have seen the faces of the representatives from the government in Geneva when they came filing in and they saw all these American citizens, there was over a hundred of us sitting there waiting, with these angry looks on our faces. And the reason they were looking the way they were looking is because they knew we knew the truth. They could fool the experts on the CERD committee because they are from all over the world, but there's American citizens! They knew we knew. So when they walked in they were like, aw, shit. And that's how they should feel every time they walk in there.

We should build this movement. The youth should know about human rights. Because the other thing it does, not only does it embarrass the government, it forces our people to think in a more worldly manner. Our people need to begin to look at international events. I'm a Pan-Africanist. I was born a Pan-African I guess. I'm watching stuff from the Continent all the time. I think African Americans in particular should be watching it. Did you know there is a new scramble for Africa? If our people had more of a sense of worldliness because we are pushing human rights, I think they would be reading, not just about Africa, but all over. And that's important. The world is small now in terms of communications. So by pushing human rights I think we require our people to step up and begin to think more broadly and look more broadly. And begin to look more broadly for remedies.

The last thing I'll say is, human rights is universal. So when we talk about human rights, it's the same human rights in Nigeria or Venezuela. The same human rights. So we are organizing with people literally all over the world using the same paradigm. And I think that's critical.

QUEEN QUET, as the first Queen Mother and official spokesperson for the Gullah/Geechee Nation, spoke on behalf of her people before the United Nations in Geneva, Switzerland. In 2008, she was recorded at UNESCO Headquarters in Paris, France at a United Nations Conference to have the human rights story of the Gullah/Geechee people archived for the United Nations. In 2009, she was invited by the Office of the High Commissioner of the United Nations to come and present before the newly founded "Minority Forum" as a representative of the Gullah/ Geechee Nation and the International Human Rights Association for American Minorities (IHRAAM). Queen Quet has won numerous awards for her scholarship, writings, artistic presentation, activism, cultural continuation and environmental preservation including: the United States Jefferson Award for community service, the Jean Laney Folk Heritage Award for Gullah Advocacy from the state of South Carolina, numerous Woman of Distinction Awards, the National Black Herstory Award, and the "Preserving Our Places in History Lifetime Achievement Award" from the South Carolina African American Heritage Commission.

DISYA WE LAND
CONTINUED
SELF-DETERMINATION OF THE GULLAH/GEECHEE NATION

QUEEN QUET
CHIEFTESS OF THE GULLAH/GEECHEE NATION[1]

The Gullah/Geechee Nation is located on the Sea Islands from Jacksonville, North Carolina southward to Jacksonville, Florida in the Atlantic Ocean and in the Lowcountry on the mainland up to the St. John's River in the United States of America. This area is the region in which numerous African ethnics groups were placed during the Transatlantic Slave trade. These Africans joined with indigenous/Native American ethnic groups. A new ethnic and linguistic national minority emerged from these people in what is now the "Gullah/Geechee Nation."

Laws within the Carolinas, Georgia, and Florida did not acknowledge nor protect the Gullah/Geechees until the Gullah/Geechees stood and fought for the "Cultural Protection Overlay District" on St. Helena Island in Beaufort County, SC which is a part of the Beaufort County Zoning District Standard Ordinance. This law is the first in the United States to actually acknowledge that Gullah culture needed to be protected by virtue of the process of zoning. The Gullah/Geechees under the guidance and leadership of the Gullah/Geechee Sea Island Coalition then proceeded to other counties in the state of South Carolina to get them to duplicate this zoning as they each proceeded with new comprehensive plans and zoning ordinances. However, these county governments would not specifically duplicate the language of this zoning and continued to allow the physical displacement of Gullah/Geechees from their homeland.

Realizing that on the local, county, and state levels that there was continued resistance to acknowledging the history of Gullah/Geechees and/or to support the continued existence of the language, "Gullah," or the continued existence of Gullah/Geechees on their own land with full use of their traditional and sacred grounds and via traditional practices, the Gullah/Geechee Sea Island Coalition which had been formed as a global grassroots organization to assist Gullah/Geechees and which had successfully worked with Gullah/Geechees of St. Helena Island to obtain the "Cultural Protection Overlay District" law, proceeded to examine other means of getting federal assistance to have the Gullah/Geechee people and their homeland protected and their traditions to continue in the Gullah/Geechee Nation.

The Gullah/Geechee Sea Island Coalition is an international grassroots organization founded in 1996 which:

• is the premiere advocacy organization for the rights of Gullah/ Geechees worldwide

• promotes and participates in the preservation of Gullah/ Geechee history, heritage, culture, and language.

• works toward Sea Island land re-acquisition and maintenance.

• celebrates Gullah/Geechee culture through artistic and educational means electronically and via "grassroots scholarship."

The Gullah/Geechee Sea Island Coalition started engagement with the International Human Rights Association for American Minorities (IHRAAM) in 1998. Marquetta L. Goodwine, who is now officially and respectfully, Queen Quet, Chieftess of the Gullah/Geechee Nation (www.QueenQuet.com) and who founded of the Gullah/Geechee Sea Island Coalition (www.gullahgeechee.net), had already been working with the United States Department of Interior's National Park Service on a special resource study for two years. She then investigated the ability of this agency to assist the Gullah/Geechees with the issues of displacement and find federal means of protection for the Gullah/Geechee land and people and their human and cultural resources on the southeastern coast. She was advised that the process required a United States congressional act.

She then approached Congressman James E. Clyburn who represented the state of South Carolina at the congressional level and he worked with the Gullah/Geechee Sea Island Coalition to craft and forward the bill to begin the "Special Resource Study of Low Country Gullah Culture." Congressman Clyburn presented this legislation to the United States Congress without success initially. While this was taking place and the Gullah/Geechees were lobbying to have their culture acknowledged as a national minority via this study process, the elders of Carolina, Georgia, and Florida continued to seek other means by which to stop the cultural degradation, exploitation, and destruction that was taking place as counties continued to allow the building of gated areas and resorts and to use eminent domain to assist with some projects as well as individuals and corporations coming in and desecrating Gullah/Geechee burial areas and gating off traditional gathering and harvesting areas while also threatening Gullah/Geechees for their land. The county tax offices assisted with Gullah/Geechee land loss by unequal taxation measures being used to cause Gullah/Geechee lands to be taxed at extreme amounts that would cause their immediate displacement as well as larger parcels of land than what would satisfy taxes due to be sold for less than fair market value. Meanwhile, Gullah/Geechee communities are not receiving educational and medical services that would equal the value of the taxes that they are paying to the counties and the states that own the educational and medical facilities placed in their communities.

Congressman Clyburn had to introduce the Gullah/Geechee special resource study legislation twice. Between the two introductions of this legislation, IHRAAM facilitated Marquetta L. Goodwine with bringing the Gullah/Geechee case before the Human Rights Commission of the United Nations on April 1, 1999. Following this introduction of the Gullah/Geechee human rights abuses to this international body, the Gullah/Geechees started a year long petition process to elect their first leader and to become a nation of their own that would be internationally recognized and would be a body that would stand to insure the protection and continuation of the Gullah/Geechee culture and all of its facets. As this petition process proceeded, the Special Resource Study of Low Country Gullah Culture was also congressionally mandated within the United States and became a process to document the existence of Gullah/Geechee culture and to evaluate whether or not this unique culture had any significance that needed acknowledgement by the United States.

On July 2, 2000, the conclusion of a year long election to have Marquetta L. Goodwine be the first leader of the Gullah/Geechees and head-of-state (in Gullah "head pun de bodee") and the official liaison and spokesperson for all Gullah/Geechees served as a public opportunity of confirmation of the ballots and the election process. The ballots had been received online and via hand written petitions that had been provided throughout the United States and online for international reach in order to insure that involvement of Gullah/Geechees that had been displaced, migrated, or were serving in the military to be able to participate if they chose to cast a ballot or submit opposition to the process. There was no opposition put forth in the year long process nor in person on July 2, 2000 at Sullivan's Island, SC in Charleston County on United States federal property. United Nations representatives were present to observe this event including representatives from IHRAAM. The United States government also had representatives present including employees of the US Department of the Interior's National Park Service. All representatives were able to speak on the program and acknowledge and agree with the process that was being undertaken.

This event was the official enstoolment of Marquetta L. Goodwine and her swearing into office. The traditional process of an enstoolment also involves a naming. Thus, Marquetta L. Goodwine became "Queen Quet, Chieftess of the Gullah/Geechee Nation" and from that day was to be the official leader of the Gullah/Geechee Nation. The Wisdom Circle Council of Elders was acknowledged and accepted by all those present via vocal vote confirmation. One year later, this body and Queen Quet returned to Sullivan's Island and presented to the world, the Gullah/Geechee Nation Constitution which built upon the mission set forth in the Gullah/Geechee Nation Declaration to "preserve, protect, and promote our history, culture, language, and homeland and to institute and demand official recognition of the governance (minority) rights necessary to accomplish our mission to take care of our community through collective efforts which will provide for the well beings of each person, and economic empowerment."

The Gullah/Geechee Nation Declaration with its mission and goals as well as a copy of the Gullah/Geechee Nation Constitution was presented to the United States National Park Service during the six year period of the Special Resource Study of Low Country Gullah Culture. The study culminated in the United States government presenting the Low Country Gullah Culture Special Resource Study and Final Environmental Impact Statement to public and to the federal government. This federal document acknowledged that "Gullah/Geechees culture is distinctive and is not yet represented and protected as an entity in the National Park System, or by any other agency." This representation and protection is the job of the Gullah/Geechee people of the Gullah/Geechee Nation with the assistance of collaborations of the local, state, and federal governments within the boundaries of the United States where Gullah/Geechees stood on their human right to self-determination as a national, linguistic, and ethnic minority. No one had previously stood to have this group acknowledged until the Gullah/Geechees began to demand the rights of their own people and they have not ceased in their demands.

The Low Country Gullah Culture Special Resource Study and Final Environmental Impact Statement clearly states:

> The Gullah/Geechee people of the Low Country and Sea Islands of South Carolina, Georgia, and Florida,

> and North Carolina are a distinctive people. They are also the only African American population of the United States with a separate, long-standing name identifying them as a separate people. They are distinct among African American peoples in this development of a tradition that depends as much upon maritime resources as upon land resources. Historically, they are speakers of the only true African American creole language of the continental United States.
>
> Gullah/Geechee people are the most African of African Americans in physical type, language, and culture; yet, they are a uniquely American cultural type formed by the fusion of African cultural heritage and American experience."
>
> The very language used seems to coincide with those of the provisions within Article 1.1(a) of the ILO Convention No. 169 in regard to "tribal people" in that tribal people are seen there as "having social, cultural and economic traditions different from other sections of the national community, identifying themselves with their ancestral territories, and regulating themselves, at least partially, by their own norms, customs, and traditions." According to the ILO, the objective elements of tribal peoples include (i) culture, social organization, economic conditions and way of life that are different from those of other segments of the national population, for example their livelihoods, language, etc.; and (ii) distinctive traditions and customs, and/or special legal recognition.[2]

The American experience acknowledged in the US federal government study was the very evolution of a national minority which is both an indigenous and tribal group of the United States which has not had its human rights, land rights, linguistic rights, or cultural rights protected by any agency of the United States government before or after this acknowledgement. Thus, the United States government confirmed for the Gullah/Geechees that they were a "national, linguistic, and ethnic minority" of the United States. This thereby furthered the efforts of internal self-determination of the Gullah/ Geechee Nation. The Gullah/ Geechee Sea Island Coalition, leaders of the Gullah/Geechee Nation, and international supporters seeking the acknowledgement of the rights of Gullah/Geechees then worked with Congressman James E. Clyburn's office to get the Gullah/Geechee Cultural Heritage Act Bill passed noting that on August 7, 2002, Congressman Clyburn wrote "Gullah Land Must be Preserved on Historic St. Helena Island":

> St. Helena Island, just off the coast of Beaufort, is steeped in African American history. It is the site where slavery was first introduced in the original 13 American colonies. It is home to Penn Center, a nationally recognized historic landmark that once served as a retreat for civil rights groups. Dr. Martin Luther King, Jr. made the initial plans for his historic march on Washington while staying there. St. Helena is the last authentic African American community in the country because its residents still retain the language and culture of their West African heritage, which we now refer to as Gullah.
>
> Forty-seven of those slave descendants had the foresight in 1920 to purchase the old Baker Plantation on St. Helena Island. Their intent was to protect their land and preserve their culture. They went to great lengths to protect their 328 acres. In 1994, they sued themselves to turn the property over to a nonprofit corporation called Lands End Woodland Club in order to keep developers from using unscrupulous methods to acquire the land.
>
> I have talked often about the legal device called partitioning, which is used to rob blacks of their property. These tactics are employed when property owners die without wills and the land is passed on to their heirs with unclear deeds. So if a buyer can convince just one of the heirs to sell his or her share, the buyer can file a legal partition and gain title to the entire parcel. I understand that now legal partition has ever failed in South Carolina.
>
> ***
>
> Unfortunately, it appears that once again the legal system will be used to deprive blacks of their rightful ownership. This is happening to slave descendants throughout the South. As the land is lost, so too is the Gullah culture that once dominated these islands. I have secured federal funding for the National Parks

> Service to study ways to prevent future loss of this important cultural heritage. However, that report due out this year, will focus on preservation and not legal reforms that are necessary to prevent this situation on St. Helena Island.
>
> There is an underlying irony that this dispute takes place in the shadow of Penn Center that has collected more than two-thousand cases of land takings from blacks. Penn Center is where blacks gathered seeking refuge from the tensions of the 60's. This is the place where the Gullah culture could thrive because its purveyors lived without any pressure to assimilate for generations. This is the place whose history was so intertwined with its people that 47 descendants of slaves sought to protect it in its natural state for eternity.
>
> It is heart wrenching to know the very legal system charged with protecting the rights of all Americans is being used to strip blacks of their rightful property ownership. If allowed to continue, the rich history and heritage that makes St. Helena so unique may be lost to future generations.

This acknowledgement by the United States Congressman of the fact that the legal system of the United States which is charged with protecting the rights of ALL Americans was being used to actually do the opposite as it related to "Blacks" who in this case are specifically Gullah/Geechees shows that even he as someone with congressional power had limited power in the true protection of Gullah/Geechee cultural and land rights. Therefore, the leaders of the Gullah/Geechee Nation have continued their efforts to insure the protection of the human rights of Gullah/Geechees.

The United States Congress voted into law the "Gullah/Geechee Cultural Heritage Act" and the law was signed by the United States President in 2006. In 2007, a 15 member commission was established to:

> 1) recognize the important contributions made to American culture and history by African-Americans known as the Gullah/Geechee who settled in the coastal counties of South Carolina, North Carolina, Florida, and Georgia; (2) assist State and local governments and public and private entities in South Carolina, North Carolina, Florida, and Georgia in interpreting the

> story of the Gullah/Geechee and preserving Gullah/Geechee folklore, arts, crafts, and music; and (3) assist in identifying and preserving sites, historical data, artifacts, and objects associated with the Gullah/Geechee for the benefit and education of the public. Provides that the Heritage Corridor shall be comprised of lands and waters depicted on a map entitled "Gullah/Geechee Cultural Heritage Corridor" dated September 2004 and on file at the National Park Service. Establishes the Gullah/Geechee Cultural Heritage Corridor Commission to assist Federal, State, and local authorities to develop and implement a management plan for Gullah/Geechee lands and waters. Sets forth the duties of the Commission, including the preparation and submission of a management plan to the Secretary of the Interior and annual reporting to the Secretary. Authorizes the Commission to make grants and enter into cooperative agreements with the States of South Carolina, North Carolina, Florida, and Georgia to prepare and implement the management plan. Provides for technical and financial assistance to the Commission. Requires the Commission to establish one or more Coastal Heritage Centers in the Heritage Corridor in accordance with the Low Country Gullah Culture Special Resource Study and Environmental Impact Study, December 2003, and additional appropriate sites. Sets forth protections for private landowners in the Heritage Corridor. Authorizes appropriations.

However, the law is clear in stating that it "Terminates the authorities under this Act 15 years after enactment." This then shows that this is not a permanent measure for the protection of the rights of Gullah/Geechees. Yet, through the process that has taken place by this commission over the last 5 years since it was seated, they have documented more than 1500 tangible and intangible resources the constitute the existence of the institutions of Gullah/Geechees that these people have had to maintain themselves in spite of any forms of protection or support from the United States or state and local governments.

The funding that was appropriated thus far via the Gullah/Geechee Cultural Heritage Act went directly to the Gullah/Geechee Cultural Heritage Commission which in turn paid the Denver Service

Center of the United States National Park Service the majority of the funds in order to complete a general management plan which shows the opinions and focal points of the most vocal commission members who do not seek to focus on human rights issues and protection of the human rights of Gullah/Geechees.

So, the result of their work has amounted to focusing on education and tourist attractions. Tourisms was the initial problem that started the major displacement of Gullah/Geechees from their homeland. The educational system continues to only acknowledge Gullah/Geechees in the context of enslavement and in some cases as the culture relates to the United States Civil Rights Movement, but does not move forward into the context of the human rights movement initiated by the Gullah/ Geechees themselves in order to insure the continued existence of their culture and the permanent ownership of lands on which they could continue their traditions and pass down the land and traditions for generations to come.

The leaders of the Gullah/Geechee Nation have been told by federal authorities and employees that the Gullah/Geechee Cultural Heritage Corridor has no land ownership or jurisdiction over land. This Corridor was created via the Gullah/Geechee Cultural Heritage Act. So, the Congressional Act in essence has no ability to insure the continuation of Gullah/Geechee culture, but has simply been a process of documentation and the storing of this documentation of tangible and intangible resources by non-Gullah/Geechee owned entities that seek to interpret the Gullah/ Geechee story through their own lens and have visitors come to their institutions to learn of the culture instead of directly placing the control of Gullah/Geechee education, rights, and economic development on the lands and waters of the Gullah/Geechee Nation into the hands of the Gullah/Geechee people. Thus, the domestic legal system is still not sufficient in protecting the rights of this linguistic, ethnic, minority that is an indigenous tribe in the southeastern United States that also has a documented Gullah/ Geechee Disapora that extends to Texas, Oklahoma, Mexico, and the Caribbean including the Bahamas.

As a result of a domestic legal remedy to turn to in spite of the federal Gullah/ Geechee Cultural Heritage Act, the Gullah/Geechees have found themselves returning to state and federal courts and agencies to:

• fight legal cases to stop the desecration of Gullah/Geechee burial areas throughout the Gullah/Geechee Nation on both private and federal lands. One such case was fought in Beaufort County, SC and won with successful use of the Declaration of the Rights of Persons Belonging to National, Ethnic, and Linguistic Minorities and invoking the rights of Gullah/Geechees based on the Gullah/Geechee Nation Constitution. This case was the Dr. White/Edding White Burial Area case regarding a Gullah/ Geechee burial area on St. Helena Island, SC. However, the National Park

Service exhumed a Gullah/Geechee burial area at Kingsley Plantation in Florida and saw no reason to contact the Gullah/Geechee Nation in regard to what they wanted to undertake. They are now using images of artifacts from this and information from this to further benefit this federally owned national historic site.

• fight legal cases against the Department of Natural Resources in North Carolina, South Carolina, Georgia, and Florida due to the continued attempt to deny Gullah/Geechee traditional fishing rights and to instead fine and jail Gullah/Geechee fishermen and confiscate their equipment. See the reports from the Environmental Defense Fund regarding efforts that continue to be underway by the Gullah/Geechee Sea Island Coalition and the Gullah/Geechee Fishing Association to fight for the rights that should belong to Gullah/Geechees to allow them to sustain themselves and their families by harvesting food from the waterways as they have done since the 1600s and to economically empower themselves by sustaining the seafood industry which also assist with insuring the quality of life in the region due to the environmental balance caused through their traditional methods of certain creatures:

http://solutions.edf.org/2010/12/07/a-voice-for-african-american-fishermen-in-the-southeast/

http://blogs.edf.org/edfish/2010/01/28/queen-quet-chieftess-of-the-gullahgeechee-nationand-edf-host-listening-session-for-gullahgeechee-fishermen/

http://blogs.edf.org/edfish/2010/03/11/listening-sessions-with-gullahgeechee-fishermencontinue/

http://blogs.edf.org/edfish/2010/04/23/last-stop-sea-breeze-nc/

• fight for legislation to stop the taxation without representation model that has been utilized to displace Gullah/Geechee families from their land even through a court procedure called "forced partition sale." Gullah/Geechees have been working to educated families about "heirs property" which is the terminology used to refer to Gullah/Geechee communal property ownership which has been breached by individuals, companies, and governmental entities over the years. Some communities have been seeking redress concerning lands that were taken by eminent domain as well.

• fight for Gullah/Geechee access to traditional and sacred areas for the gathering of natural herbs and sweetgrass or to have traditional ceremonies and access to waterways is an on-going problem and there is no one identifiable court or agency to deal with these matters. Thus, Gullah/Geechees find themselves discouraged seeking to find out who should be charged with protecting their rights in regard to these.

Special protection is a need that has been discussed at the United Nations Forum on Minority Rights which the leaders of the Gullah/Geechee Nation have participated in as another attempt to seek the necessary tools and connections to insure that their rights are protected and international recognized before their people are displaced or further forced into assimilation. The IACHR and the Forum on Minority Rights have all acknowledged that the need for special protection arises from the greater vulnerability of indigenous, tribal, and minority groups because of their historical conditions of marginalization and discrimination. In its 1972 Resolution on "Special Protection for Indigenous Populations: Action to Combat Racism and Racial Discrimination," the IACHR held that "for historical reasons and because of moral and humanitarian principles, special protection for indigenous populations constitutes a sacred commitment of the states." The IACHR sees a central component of this being that a:

> recognition that ensuring the full and effective enjoyment of human rights by indigenous peoples requires consideration of their particular historical, cultural, social and economic situation and experience. In most instances, this has included identification of the need for special measures by states to compensate for the exploitation and discrimination to which these societies have been subjected at the hands of the non-indigenous.[3]

The Gullah/Geechee Nation's citizens seek to have the full enjoyment of their human rights so that they can insure their own measures of fulfillment of their fundamental freedoms, without restrictions, and full effectiveness of their own social, economic, and cultural rights. This is apparent in the Gullah/Geechee Nation Constitution which was done in order to insure safeguards to their physical and cultural survival on the Sea Islands and Lowcountry from Jacksonville, NC to Jacksonville, FL. However, the United States has not provided any special protection to the Gullah/Geechee Nation and its citizens to insure their property rights over their ancestral lands and their natural resources. So, they continue to engage with various legal entities and governmental bodies regarding this matter.

Gullah/Geechee culture is inextricably tied to the land. So, without continued access to the lands and waterways and the opportunity to continue traditional practices on the land and in the waterways without threat of fines and imprisonment or threat to life due to hostile approaches by people in gated areas or that have encroached into Gullah/ Geechee communities, the special relationship that Gullah/Geechees have with the land would cease. This places the continuation of this unique national, linguistic, ethnic indigenous tribal group in jeopardy. Documenting the existence of the culture into extinction or to assist others to further exploit the culture by using its name to promote tourism is not beneficial to assisting with preventing this on-slaught that Gullah/ Geechees came together to prevent from taking place.

Gullah/Geechees are not simply fighting for their land and waterways for material subsistence, but for spiritual and cultural reasons and the integrity of their people. If it is agreed, that "culture is the highest social and historical expression of spiritual development" and that man has a duty to preserve, practice, and foster culture, by every means within its power, then Gullah/Geechees have a right to do this for their own culture like any other people in the world without having new entities of nonGullahGeechees or assimilated Gullah/Geechees presented to them to dictate how their story should be told or how their lands should be governed even if that process will further their displacement.

> The lack of access to land and natural resources can produce conditions of extreme poverty for the affected indigenous communities, given that the lack of possession of, and access to, their territories prevents them from using and enjoying the natural resources that they need to obtain the good necessary for their subsistence, develop their traditional cultivation, hunting, fishing or gathering activities, access traditional health systems, and other key socio-cultural functions. Therefore, the lack of access to ancestral territories, and the lack of State action in this regard, expose indigenous and tribal people to precarious or sub-human living conditions in the fields of access to food, water, dignified housing, basic utilities and health, and consequently bear an impact-inter alia-upon higher rates of child and infant mortality and malnutrition, and higher vulnerability to illnesses and epidemics. To that extent, the State's lack of guarantee of indigenous and tribal peoples' right to live in their ancestral territory may imply subjecting them to situations of extreme

> unprotectedness, which entail violations of their rights to life, to personal integrity, to a dignified existence, to food, to water, to health, to education and children's rights, among others. In addition, disregard for the rights of the members of indigenous communities over their ancestral territories can affect, for the same causes, other basic rights, such as the right to cultural identity, the collective right to cultural integrity, or the right to collective survival of communities and their members. The extreme living conditions borne by the members of the indigenous communities that lack access to their ancestral territory cause them to suffer, and undermine the preservation of their way of life, customs and language.[4]
>
> Inter-American jurisprudence has characterized indigenous territorial property as a form of property whose foundation lies not in official state recognition, but in the traditional use and possession of the land and resources; indigenous and tribal people's territories 'are theirs by right of their ancestral use or occupancy. The right to indigenous communal property is also grounded in indigenous legal cultures, and in their ancestral ownership systems, independent of state recognition; the origin of indigenous and tribal peoples' property rights is, therefore, also found in the customary system of land tenure that has traditional existed among the communities.[5]

The Gullah/Geechee Nation territory has consisted of Gullah/Geechee family compounds on the same lands acknowledged by William Tecumseh Sherman's Special Field Order 15 [http://www.history.umd.edu/Freedmen/sfo15.htm] which was a United States federal field order issued in January of 1865 after which the removal of Gullah/Geechees from these lands during the Jim Crow era in the United States was allowed via displacements caused by taxation, death threats, deaths, and forced partition sales brought on to allow property to be used by non-Gullah/Geechees and government entities and agencies. Thus, the citizens of the Gullah/Geechee Nation have sought to remedy this through internal self-determination and have consistently sought various means to do so on the local, state, federal, and international levels.

Much of the lack of assistance of the part of the United States governmental agencies and commissions is due to fear of threat if they use international law mechanisms as well as a lack of knowledge by courts of rights that stem from ancestral use and possession, the lack of traditional rights laws for Gullah/Geechees, and continued "title clearance" issues that family compound owners are faced with in courts because Gullah/Geechees have been forced to be placed within non-indigenous municipalities that are within the Gullah/Geechee Nation. Thus, other laws tend to thwart individual efforts put forth by Gullah/ Geechees or Gullah/Geechee families when taken to court to protect their land, water, and fishing rights.

The very right to life of the Gullah/Geechee population depends on their ability to have power to have a unique system of rights recognized within the area from Jacksonville, NC to Jacksonville, FL. This should allow for protection of continued land use for building in traditional family compound patterns, traditional agricultural uses, traditional gathering practices and use of herbs for healing and cooking, traditional hunting practices, traditional gathering of items for craft and utilitarian uses such as in the case of sweetgrass baskets, and traditional seafood harvesting practices including fishing, shrimping, oyster picking, clam digging. However, the leaders of the Gullah/ Geechee Nation only see these things being insured if Gullah/Geechee traditionalists are those that are part of the decisions made regarding their cultural and natural resources. Academicians and politicians are not those whose livelihoods are directly affected by the lack of access to these resources. However, the majority of Gullah/Geechees are affected in this way. This majority has to not only contend with the physical and mental health declines that have taken place due to this attack on their region and accessibility to things that previously kept them strong physically, mentally, spiritually, and culturally, they also have to deal with environmental damaged caused by outside people destroying the natural environment via their building patterns and over fishing as well as pollution and climate change. The stresses of these things have a detrimental effect on the Gullah/Geechees and thereby are decreasing their quality of life, especially in the urbanized areas of the Gullah/Geechee Nation.

The leaders of the Gullah/Geechee Nation see a need to have the United States provide measures to reverse these detrimental effects on the people and the environment of the Gullah/Geechee Nation. This can only be done in direct consultation with the leaders of the Gullah/Geechee Nation who are the ones that have continued to stand for human rights and seek to negotiate on behalf of Gullah/Geechees worldwide. There are measures that can be immediately put into effect to suspend some actions that would further deteriorate the culture and the community in which it has evolved and thrive and measures should be put in place to their repair the damages that have been done and prevent any further damage through projects that threaten the physical or cultural survival of Gullah/Geechees. This cannot be done when there are not mechanisms "on the books" that the United States or the states of North Carolina, South Carolina, Georgia, or Florida see that they are to adhere to. This also cannot be done by non-profit entities being put in place to seek grants on their own in order to attempt to fund projects that communities will seek as valuable. A direct funding resource provided to Gullah/Geechees is necessary for this to be effective and sustaining. The Gullah/Geechee Nation's leaders are still at the forefront of making sure that these arrangements come to fruition so that Gullah/Geechee culture will remain in the Gullah/Geechee Nation for generations to come because "disya da we land!"

ENDNOTES

1 Gullah/Geechee Nation, Post Office Box 1109, St. Helena Island SC 29920 <http://www.gullahgeecheenation.com>

2 ILO, "Indigenous & Tribal Peoples' Rights in Practice-A Guide to ILO Convention No. 169." Programme to Promote ILO Convention No. 169 (PRO 169), International Labor Standards Department 2009, p.9.

3 IACHR, Report No. 75/02, Case 11.140, Mary and Carrie Dann (United States), December 27, 2002, par. 125. IACHR, Report No. 40/04, Case 12.053, Maya Indigenous Communities of the Toledo District (Belize), Octover 12, 2004, par. 95.

4 "Indigenous and Tribal Peoples' Rights Over the Ancestral Lands and Natural Resources: Norms and Jurisprudence of the Inter-American Human Rights System OEA/SER.L/VII.Doc. 56/09 2010, p. 22.

5 "Indigenous and Tribal Peoples' Rights Over the Ancestral Lands and Natural Resources: Norms and Jurisprudence of the Inter-American Human Rights System OEA/SER.L/VII.Doc. 56/09 2010, p. 26.

DR. Y. N. KLY (1935-2011) sought to advance the cause of oppressed peoples not only through UN human rights assemblies, but also through tribunals such as the Human Rights Committee and the Inter-American Court: Gullah-Geechees, African Americans, Kashmiris, Thlingit, Dalits, Lil'wat, Apsalookas, Puerto Ricans, and others. As a Professor Emeritus in political science and international law at the University of Regina, and as a founder and primary theoretician directing IHRAAM, he brought unique and far-reaching insights into the possible conduct of domestic and international affairs. His many books dealing with the rights of oppressed minorities, and in particular his own African American and Gullah-Geechee peoples, sought to advance an understanding of their actual politico-legal situation within multinational states, and the many legal and institutional means and route to improving their socio-economic well being without surrendering their unique and beautiful cultures. He sought to move the UN itself towards a fuller understanding and institutional protection of Article 1 of both of the major human rights treaties, which legally enshrined the right to self-determination, by means of two international conferences held in Geneva. He was two-time winnder of the prestigious "Outstanding Books Award" from the Gustavus Myers Center for Human Rights for his books, *International Law & the Black Minority in the US* (2000) and *A Popular Guide to Minority Rights* (2005), see excerpt, left.

MINORITY RIGHTS
Some Questions & Answers

Y. N. KLY & DIANA KLY

QUESTION: Why should African-Americans look to international human rights law for help achieving equal status and equality in America?

International human rights law promotes norms of minority treatment that are more wide-ranging and have been more successful in practice than limited concept of civil rights (nonOdiscrimination and equality before the law, which in the United States is interpreted to mean the same treatment). These norms reflect the modern world's experience in trying to accommodate the problems of minorities by giving the historically evolved situation and circumstances of the minority group adequate consideration, leading often to positive state action and different treatment, in view of their different requirements.

Viewing the problem of minorities within the international context prevents the error of thinking that local minorities' problems are unique (and hence insoluble). By enabling the African-American problem to be viewed within the context of a whole range of problems which have typically arisen for minorities worldwide—by the mere fact of their being a minority—we can see that African-Americans' development problems are essentially caused by the fact that they are a minority in a state that refuses to recognize or provide for their minority rights or to permit any form of community control. Segregation attempted to institute the cultural assimilation of African-Americans while maintaining their physical separation.

QUESTION: International human rights law as a model for minority rights is all well and good, but who says America will pay any attention?

Political pressure created by African-Americans demanding these rights, in conjunction with international pressure, will create circumstances that will raise the cost both domestically as well as internationally, of denial of these rights beyond the benefit of not providing for them. To maintain the creditability of its position as a leading power, the United States must provide for minority rights, should these rights be demanded. As a matter of fact, in cases where effective demands are made by Native Americans, we have seen positive action on the part of the United States government. Faced with an effective contingent of Native American lobbyists from the United Sates and politically forced to respond in an internationally supported forum concerning the needs of the world's indigenous peoples, the United States delegate to the United Nations Working Group on Indigenous Populations was forced to respond, according to the UNPO Monitor, that:

> ...although human rights of indigenous people is promoted in the United States, the promotion of the rights of dignity and "equality" are not sufficient. Expressed support of the basic goals of the draft Declaration [on the Rights of Indigenous Peoples]. Offered a working model on how the rights of indigenous people can be recognized and implemented—on the right to self-determination, raised the issue of the recognition of tribal self-governance and autonomy over a broad range of issues as a positive development in the national level. Highlighted the uniqueness of this concept of self-governance which considers a "government-to-government relationship." Finally, expressed determination to explore how this concept of self-determination might be translated into international terms.

Paradoxically, one of the strongest arguments for the effectiveness of the international human rights treaties is the general reluctance of states to ratify them and hence become subject to their jurisdiction. The United States, for example, for all its bravado about being the most powerful, most independent state, for decades was afraid to ratify more than the Genocide Convention. Y.N. Kly has argued, in *The Anti-Social Contract,* that such reluctance stems from the fear that its domestic minorities, African-Americans in particular, will thereby be made aware of and given the incentive to demand this internationally-recognized right.

Only recently has the United States ratified the International Covenant on Civil and Political Rights (ICCPR) and at that, it has hedged its ratification in a forest of reservations, understandings, and declarations. Most particularly, it has refrained from ratifying the first Optional Protocol, which would permit groups and individuals (as opposed to states) to take human rights grievances to the Human Rights Committee, which monitors state adherence to the ICCPR. The United States has yet to ratify the International Covenant on Economic, Social and Cultural Rights, the International Convention on the Elimination of All Forms of Racial Discrimination (CERD), the International Convention on the Suppression and Punishment of the Crime of Apartheid, the Convention against Torture and Other Cruel, Inhuman or Degrading Treatment or Punishment, or even the Convention on the Rights of Child—to name but a few. Why such hesitancy, if there were not the fear of the obligations incurred thereby, which might be too politically expensive to resist.

A state's ratification of the human rights treaties brings along with it the obligation to report to the United Nations on its human rights practices, and to have its reports questioned by the various states' representatives of the treaties concerned.

Non-governmental organizations (NGOs) have the right to submit communications concerning these State Reports, communications which may provide documented information on human rights violations by the state.

Criticism by state representatives in human rights forums and tribunals becomes fodder for the world public opinion and permits the exertion of constant pressure on states which don't abide by their obligation to enforce internationally protected rights.

QUESTION: It is often said that the United Nations depends heavily upon American financial support for its very existence. How, then, can the UN act effectively against the hand that feeds it?

First, a serious observation of the decisions reached by the UN over a period of the past 30 years does not support the assumption that the UN will not reach decisions contrary to the will of the United States. Indeed, the evidence against the assumption is so overwhelming that we only need to examine UN decisions in almost any area: law of the sea, decolonization, human rights, the embargo of Cuba, etc.

Most major African-American leaders have known that, in order to be successful, the African American struggle to achieve equality within America must be internationalized. Today, there is no other mechanism un existence which permits a group to internationalize their struggle except the UN. All minority movements go there—if for no other reason than the UN is the crossroads where the world meets and makes decisions which come to represent the moral ad legal authority of world opinion. As a pivotal arena of public opinion and thereby political power, the UN forces states to be concerned about its views. No state (nor indeed any serious liberation movement) questions its value—although they may attempt to devalue it because they fear its power or criticism.

IHRAAM African-American Delegates to the UN report that the UN is full of diplomats in inter-governmental and governmental capacity who harbor good will towards the African-American cause. But they can do nothing if African-Americans themselves do nothing. UN diplomats themselves understand that the credibility of their human rights program itself could be severely called into question if it should appear that they were willing to address the African-American plight because of the power of the United States. And United States diplomats in turn realize that their road is made harder, every time they wish to press an issue with a state, if they can be countered in turn with the issue of their treatment of African-Americans at home.

QUESTION: Haven't African-Americans tried to pursue their human rights—unsuccessfully—through the UN before?

No. The human rights machinery of the UN is a recent development. Past efforts were never processed or followed through. Since its inception, the United Nations has been viewed as a focus of appeal by numerous aggrieved nationalities who have been stymied in their attempts to achieve adequate response to their grievances through domestic legal systems. However, all too frequently, the groups concerned are unaware of the legal and political conditions and processes which will enable the United Nations to consider their complaints. Trips to Geneva are made, important contacts are spoken to, good will is expressed, and well-documented grievances exchange hands. And yet, because the necessary political and legal processes are not followed (or did not exist), it is as if nothing had been done at all—even though the minority/nationality representatives concerned may in all sincerity feel that they have taken their group's grievances to the UN.

Many African-Americans are under the misappre-hension that their grievances have already been successfully submitted (maybe even numerous times) to the United Nations. But this is not so. The most noteworthy of such instances is that of the "We Charge Genocide" petitioners, a distinguished body of African-Americans, Dr. W.E.B. DuBois among them, who addressed their complaint to the General Assembly in 1951. At the time of this petition, the UN was under the sway of the "impossibility to act" doctrine which asserted the unlimited sovereignty of states over their citizens, and states' rights to noninterference in domestic affairs as it related to gross violation of human rights, apart from genuine threat to world peace. (This doctrine has now been overcome.) Also, as above-mentioned, short of a threat to world peace, there were no legal procedures within the UN that would have permitted it to respond to such a communication. At that time, the United States had not yet ratified the Genocide Convention, nor the International Covenant on Civil and Political Rights, with its minority protection article (27). A cardinal principle of international law is that a state is not bound by a treaty to which it is not a party. ECOSOC's Resolution 1503 (XLVIII) concerning gross violations of human rights, enacted in May, 1970, had not yet come into force.

While the National Conference of Black Lawyers submitted a complaint through the 1503 procedure in 1979, their complaint was not accepted by the Working Group of the Sub-Commission, and thus was not given to the Sub-Commission.

This may be due to problems deriving from political pressures in the Sub-Commission from the United States and its numerous allies, or the fact that the UN's minority rights law was not as fully developed as it is today (Special Rapporteur Francesco Capotorti's study had not yet been received, nor had the 1992 Declaration on Minorities been adopted, nor had the Human Rights Committee released its General Comment interpreting Article 27 as requiring positive measures of minority protection on the part of states, etc.)

Now, however, there is an extensive body of international legal instruments available in support of international legal argumentation for minority rights, and there are African-American experts in international law undertaking action on various levels, from complaint procedure to information provision to the various Committees monitoring the UN treaties, to conflict warning. Through the International Human Rights Association of American Minorities (IHRAAM), an African-American-launched international NGO awarded consultative status with the

Economic and Social Council of the United Nations in 1992, United States minority issues are being presented to the UN Commission on Human Rights and other UN organs.

Now, through IHRAAM, African-American groups have a means of direct and official input to the UN.

QUESTION: You know, frankly, I'm tired of being referred to as a belonging to a "minority." No matter how you shake it, the word itself makes you feel as if minority people are somehow less important than majority people.

For the purposes of international legal protection, the term minority is essentially an international legal construct, like victim, accused, plaintiff, etc., in domestic law. It need not relate directly with how peoples refer to themselves or how they are referred to in the domestic constitutional-legal documents of states. Hence in the Philippines, the term "cultural communities" has been used. Romania has used the term "co-inhabiting nationality," etc. This was a way of addressing the fact that the term "minority" had itself become debased, and was synonymous with various forms of inequality between "the majority" and "the minority," because the term "minority" specified a category of citizens whose overall position in the state is less strong than that of the majority ethny.

While negotiations between minorities and states might lead to the substitution of other terms for that of "minority," at the present time it is appropriate to refer to minority when approaching the issue of minority rights in international law, because this is the international legal terminology in which international law presently frames the rights of non-dominant groups living in multi-national states.

QUESTION: What are minority rights in international law?

Minority rights are the rights of persons belonging to non-dominant nations, communities, groups, etc. living in the same state, exercised individually and in community with members of their group. While these rights include the right to non-discrimination and equality before the law, they also include the right to be different and to exercise appropriate degrees of autonomy as required for equal status.

The intent of minority rights is to protect and preserve the unique ethnic, cultural and religious identities of minorities, and to facilitate their equal status development. In order to accomplish this, most multi-national states have evolved, in addition to non-discrimination and equality before the law, a wide range of proactive practices, including politico-legal structures permitting minority autonomy in various socio-economic fields such as education, health, culture, criminal justice, welfare, etc.

QUESTION: How do minority rights differ from civil rights?

From the perspective of providing for protection from oppression by the dominant group, which usually controls the apparatus of the state in which both live, minority rights are human rights and are therefore inherently held by minorities both on an individual and a collective basis. The ultimate responsibility for their interpretation and implementation lies with the international tribunals, agencies, the UN, other states, etc. Civil rights authority resides in the legislation and case law of the state (usually controlled by the majority ethny) and they are the final judge and jury as to its interpretation and implementation. However, civil rights is often used to implement human rights domestically so that citizens need not go to the international tribunals for remedy. Where this is largely successful, for all purposes, civil rights, and minority rights are the same.

While valuable, civil rights is fundamentally a general right which functions as if all citizens were the same. It asserts the right of persons belonging to minorities to freedom from discrimination, but not to positive entitlements which promote minority equal status with the majority.

QUESTION: Why hasn't civil rights worked?

As a minority in a majoritarian democratic system (as opposed to a pluralist system), African-Americans don't have the voting power to enforce adequate consideration of their needs. American electoral procedures such as the single non-transferable vote (as opposed to proportional representation) and at large municipal voting (as opposed to the ward system) are all geared to ensure majority domination.

However, even if African-Americans were to vote under a system which gave them full representation according to their voting numbers, insofar as they are a numeric minority, they could still continue to be outvoted on every issue where their interest might clash with that of the majority. There would still be no (institutionalized) way which ensured that the system would address their specific needs or permit African-American communities to address their needs, themselves.

QUESTION: Surely, if individual African-Americans are elected to office, this should mean greater clout for the community?

While African-Americans holding elected office doubtless feel strong obligations to their community and project their concerns in whatever arenas they may be functioning in, such officials also have obligations to the other communities over whom they also have jurisdiction. Frequently, in fact, elected black leaders have operated what Cynthia Enloe, writing with regard to black Americans, terms a sub-machine:

> a patronage and favor-dispensing organ nominally controlled by a politician from a relatively weak ethnic group [whose] own influence and resources depend on access to the resources of the larger machine controlled by politicians of another community. In essence, the sub-machine boss is the loyal lieutenant of the machine boss; but he is permitted enough autonomy to build a personal power base of his own so long as it never rivals that the senior patron.

These representatives, while they may be African-American, cannot be seen to be speaking for the African-American communities. Their position is therefore very ambiguous where the interests of majority and minority conflict. While a number of mayors in major American cities are now African-American, in many instances it cannot be said that the African-American communities that have elected them have benefited. So the question remains: who has the legitimacy and authority, as conferred by the democratic process, to speak for African-Americans? Is there a need for an African-American election? Are African-Americans enjoying democracy in America, or have their interests and needs, insofar as they differ from that of the majority population, been consistently submerged by the interest of the majority Anglo-American ethny? Is the subordination of African-American need to majority interest even visible in the very court decisions which enforced their civil rights since, as Derrick Bell has observed, "Successful court decisions in relation to civil rights coincide with those case decisions that also serve to benefit the majority ethny even more"?

QUESTION: Were we misdirected when we struggled for civil rights and against the "separate but equal" doctrine?

No. At the time, there really wasn't much understanding of discussion of the options (nor indeed, was conventional international law as developed with regard to minority rights as at present). Resistance to segregation, the American version of apartheid, and indeed, the image of apartheid and Bantustans as practiced in South Africa, may have weighed against the maintenance of separate institutions, in the presumption that they would necessarily be controlled by Anglo-Americans and thus kept unequal. However, the African-American people may not have generally understood that what may have appeared as the alternate process, "integration," was in reality assimilation, and would encourage the dismantling of the existing degree of African-American economic, political and educational institutions, communities, families, etc.

Most important to note is that African-Americans were neither separate nor equal. The doctrine, while using the words "separate but equal" was actually a doctrine of segregation and racism. All institutions of the African-American community were under the indirect control of the Anglo-American majority ethny through the apparatus of the state: school curricula, the justice system, the licensing system for professionals, etc. Thus, African-Americans have never fought for nor against a separate but equal system. They have fought against racist (Anglo-American) oppression and for civil rights, assuming that civil rights was the way of overcoming Anglo-American oppression, while racism was simply the tool to maintain the oppression.

While African-Americans may have brought about the end of official constitutional-legal discrimination (segregation), they have not achieved equal status (particularly as a group) in the electoral system, or indeed, in terms of general level of political and economic control in any sector. So while the struggle for civil rights (the rights of a citizen) has been valuable, it has not provided equality or equal status in law or in fact. It has provided for African-Americans to be treated the same as Anglo-Americans regardless of whether this "same" treatment leads to greater inequality in fact or not, and regardless of whether treating African-Americans as the same legally produces greater or lesser legal equality. It provided for their cultural and political assimilation into the Anglo-American underclass, for their disappearance as a separate nation; in short, it provided for ethnocide.

QUESTION: Does non-discrimination (equality before the law) work for African-Americans?

Apart from marginal remedy for some individuals, not at all, because most discrimination is institutional, structural and systemic. The main recourse provided by equality (same treatment) before the law/non-discrimination is threat of court action. As any who have ever undertaken such legal action can testify, it is a tremendously costly and lengthy process, with the outcomes always uncertain and the proofs concerning individual situations burdened by subtleties often beyond the power of the courts to capture. While successful lawsuits likely do cause some attitudinal discrimination to abate, it is likely that attitudinal discrimination is pushed underground, while systemic discrimination remains, disguised in legitimate institutions, politico-legal mandates, prerogatives and necessities.

A further problem with attempting to solve discrimination problems through the courts is the fact that, increasingly, the United States judicial system regards equal treatment "of rich and poor alike" as before mentioned, to mean the same treatment (in abstract, making these two unequals equal in such a way as to seem concerned rather with preventing the possibility of discrimination against the rich) and thereby discounts factors that differentiate the parties concerned, such as poverty, historic oppression, etc.

Constant litigation on the part of aggrieved individuals is not the solution but remains a symptom of the problem, which is systemic and institutional.

QUESTION: If non-discrimination laws don't end discrimi-nation, how do you end discrimination?

First we should consider some of the sources and purposes of discrimination. Discrimination does not derive from a free-floating attitude of "racism" arising spontaneously in the minds of some "bad people" who "don't like [black] people."

Typically it evolves dialectically through specific historical events leading to the creation of systemically generated and ensured inequalities, whether its concerns today's third world economic refugees, victims of the neo-colonial international economic order, or the situation of the African-Americans, victims of a long history of one nation's official systemic policies devoted to ensuring the dominance of Anglo-Americans. The material and psycho-social hierarchies generated by systemic inequality in turn condition a web of attitudes, fears, distastes, and hostilities.

However, awareness of this systemic causality plays little part in most inter-group relations—not just because of the complexity of the understanding required, but also because what is really at issue is not just majority distaste for this or that trait of the discriminated group. The issue is collective power relations between the groups, and the individual power of group members that either benefits or suffers from this unequal relation. These are pocketbook issues and concerns "having" (as opposed to "sharing" which can be properly viewed as "having an appropriate part of," or negatively viewed as "having less," or at minimum as "maximizing your losses," insofar as failure to share may result in a situation in which the pie itself is destroyed.) It concerns habits of interaction, customary

The true problematic of African American liberation.
from *The Black Book II: From Hajji Malik Al-Shabazz to Barack Obama* by Dr. Y. N. Kly

assumptions and so on, all of which are measured on a scale of relative privilege.

Psycho-spiritual complexes deriving from the long history of official systemic discrimination and gross human rights violation in which African-Americans have been subjected, lead any in the majority culture to take it for granted that they should receive priority consideration over African-Americans in the allocation of social benefits, i.e. jobs, education, housing. Many, while refusing to admit the relevance of historical/systemic factors to the present day African-American condition, consciously and unconsciously anticipate and fear retaliation for their disproportionate privileges. Few can be impervious to the distorted and inflammatory depictions of African-Americans in the major American media, or indeed the reality of their disproportionately negative standing in all typical Anglo-American measurements of social well-being (income, life expectancy, health, education, etc.) Such a web of motivation often leads the majority population to a reluctance to surrender any of the advantages and privileges which have been directly tied to its historical role as victimizer. Far better to blame the victim than to admit or dwell on causal factors which could lead to its recognition of both the justice, need and wisdom of surrendering its position of superiority, both material and attitudinal, which translates into the proportionate sharing of political and economic power and resources.

Equally, the remediation of such ingrained attitudes and long term abuse as has existed in the African-American case might require not merely the alleviation of material inequality, but also a form of public repentance as exemplified by an official admission of and apology/reparations for the history of systemic discrimination and gross human rights violations.

Once a measure of equal status has been established between groups, any tendency to discriminate would likely lose its deep-rooted and destructive basis, and where it remained, become similar to the milder rivalries and frictions which exist between cultures which nonetheless recognize each other's full human equality, e.g. the rivalry between the British and French, etc. It is in such cases that non-discrimination and recourse to the courts is most effective. However, in situations where the historical situation has led to deep and pervasive structural inequalities in the relationship between majority and minority, the effectiveness of policies of non-discrimination for creating equality are negligible.

So the question is one rather of establishing equal-status and interdependence between groups.

Within the American framework, the notion of how

nondiscrimination policy can succeed in producing equality probably goes something like this: if every instance of discrimination is prevented, then discrimination as a whole will be ended, and thus meritorious individuals, who exist in similar proportions in all groups, will rise to their natural place in the general social order, and hence all groups, by natural process, will end up having a proportionate share of the social product, and a proportionate standing in all social indicators, i.e. equality.

This view of non-discrimination is concerned, not so much with protecting the right to be different, as with insisting that difference not be noticed or not matter, when it comes to allocating benefits, etc. Inactuality, it becomes a game of "let's pretend": let's pretend that the controller (the employer, the landlord, the banker, the real estate broker, the university professor) doesn't notice that you are a minority member; he/she will treat you as if he thought you were equal (the same as an Anglo-American) although actual social conditions and prejudicial Anglo-American social criteria may lead him/her to assume (rightly or wrongly) that the schools you attended as a child were under-financed, that the community your grew up in and presently live in is beset by social problems resulting from unemployment, underemployment or low-wage employment, that your ability to excel or even function in the job may be impaired by the whole gamut of social factors which beset you as a member of a devalued group, thereby rendering you less capable, less reliable, and so on. This not only leads inescapably to hypocrisy, but is also highly insulting. Insofar as the collective identity of the minority is burdened by stigma, so is the standing of the individual, whether the attendant presumptions apply to him/her or not. There is no way for individuals to completely, or even sufficiently, escape the stigma attached to the collective identity even if they do manage to escape the material conditions. In short, the game of pretending to ignore differences is a way of suggesting that there is something wrong with being different (non-Anglo-American): a way of imposing cultural domination and ignoring your right to be who you are, with equal status.

Non-discrimination can only be achieved by ensuring the right to be different by whatever means that may require. It may require both an attempt to put a stop to negative action, as well as taking positive action on behalf of preserving the identity and promoting the equality of discriminated-against groups through politic0-legal or socio-economic policies directed specifically towards the group concerned.

QUESTION: Maybe discrimination is rooted in human nature and can't be prevented?

This is unlikely. Most research shows that the source of discrimination lies in a historical oppression or devaluation which is systemically implemented and ensured by the state. Thus, it can only be appealed against to the state that is also its creator and preserver. As far as minority rights are concerned, the key may lie in sidestepping the issue of discrimination; in getting equally through minority control of institutions, and leaving prejudice to its most natural correction: the development of respect and esteem deriving from equal-status relations and the creation of situations of interdependence among groups.

Discrimination counts most and is maintained when one group has to go to another group which is prejudiced against it for fulfillment of basic needs: shelter, housing, education, capital; that is, when one group is made dependent on another, and when the law of that group comes to feel that they are superior to the dominated group, and that there is something wrong with any number of aspects of the dependent group. If African-Americans run their own communities, their own socio-economic institutions, then they no longer have to try to achieve their needs in and through socio-economic institutions (etc.) controlled by the Anglo-American community. They are then able to provide for their own through initiatives enabled by access to proportionate share of the public purse (i.e. tax revenue, etc.), thus creating conditions of interdependence between groups, enabling the marginalization of the problem of discrimination.

QUESTION: Aren't rights or measures that are just for minorities a kind of reverse discrimination?

No. The concept of reverse discrimination as used in the United States is an effective way of attempting to ignore the existence of minorities and minority rights, and psychologically prevent minorities from seeking rights outside of their control. It suggests that the historical situation of the dominant group is the same as that of the devalued minority, and that where there is no difference, no right to be different, all should be treated the same—even if the effects maintain inequality for the minority. International law specifically militates against the concept of reverse discrimination. See Article 1:4 of the Convention on the Elimination of All Forms of Racial Discrimination (CERD) and 8:3 of the Declaration on the Rights of Persons Belonging to National or Ethnic, Religious, and Linguistic Minorities.

QUESTION: Do special measures and special rights apply to all minorities? What about homosexuals, or the disabled? What about Greek or Irish Americans?

Minority rights are essentially collective rights as they exist for the purpose of eliminating minority oppression and inequality. Therefore in a technical sense, the word "minority" and the word "victim" in domestic law become similar when the right to international protection is evoked. It is evoked because some important aspect of the minority's rights and needs is being denied, ignored or trampled upon by the majority. Customary international law suggests that rights involved in Article 27 of the ICCPR, as far as the United States is concerned, apply particularly to the national minorities: the African-Americans, Native Americans, and Chicanos. These minorities existed collectively within the state as the time it was constituted, and are not seen as immigrants from another state within the international system.

Immigrant minorities, on the other hand, have made individual choices to leave duly constituted states in which they were citizens; there is implicit in the notion of immigration, the acceptance on the part of the immigrant of the desire to assimilate. This does not mean, however, that the state may not be willing to accord them certain resources or special rights. Canada, for instance, has such a multicultural policy which benefits its many immigrant minorities. This does not put them on the same plane, however, as Canada's national minorities, the aboriginal peoples and the French Canadians, who either enjoy or are recognized to have the right to significantly greater politico-legal control of socio-economic and cultural institutions, and who seek to be regarded in full equality as founding nations of the state.

Social minorities (gays, the disabled, women [so-defined because of their non-dominant position], etc.) do not figure within the configuration of national or ethnic, religious and linguistic minorities protected by international minority rights law.

However, other human rights law applies to them.

QUESTION: What is the difference between special measures and special rights?

While special measures refer to measures taken on behalf of the group which cease to exist once the minority achieves equal status with the majority, special rights are permanent and are accorded with a view to recognizing the minority's right to remain different, to continue to exist and develop as a minority or nationality distinct from the majority culture, while interacting with it on a basis of equality and interdependence.

Special rights may include the notion of proportionality, widely recognized as effective for reducing group conflict and ensuring equal development. It may be introduced in a limited manner (e.g. in only some sectors such as hiring in the civil service) or extensively in most public jurisdictions. IN Switzerland, for example, the French, German and Italian populations share federal executive, legislative and judicial positions proportionally; proportionality is even taken into account in the armed forces. In Belgium of the 1950's-60's, a near 50-50 form of proportionality was extensively used. Belgium's 1971 constitution stipulated that with the possible exception of the prime minister, the cabinet must comprise an equal number of Flemish and French ministers. The same devotion to the principle of equality is also found in Belgian government's allocation of resources. When railway lines had to be abandoned, when industrial development projects were sited and financed, when road were built, the decisions were made on the basis of equal shares in the benefits for each nationality or minority.

In particular, special rights creates pluralist democracy in order to assure equal status of all nations or minorities in the state—minority control of institutions in various sectors, such as education, healthcare, the justice system, culture, welfare, tourism, etc. Control over these sectors, whether achieved through autonym, devolution, federalism, etc. permit minority control over important elements affecting its well being and daily life. This allows the minority a measure of self-determination without threatening the territorial integrity of the state.

QUESTION: Can we talk about self-determination and not be talking about secession?

Yes. Self-determination has come to be divided in scholarly discourse between external self-determination (the right of a group to secede and become fully politically independent) and internal self-determination (where a group exercises political rights, among them the right to control over jurisdictions of social activity such as education, health, criminal justice, etc. in varying degrees, while remaining within the existing state).

QUESTION: In Article 1 of both Covenants, self-determination is said to be the right of "peoples." Is self-determination a minority right, too?

Many scholars such as Ian Brownlie argue that trying to establish differences between groups such as "peoples," "minorities" and" indigenous peoples" and their respective rights is fruitless, insofar as the issues are the same, and "the segregation of topics is an impediment to fruitful work." In his keynote address to the Hamline Conference on African-Americans and the Right to Self-Determination reprinted herein, Dr. Kly further advances these arguments. In practice, varying degrees of internal self-determination have been accorded to both peoples and national minorities in order to promote harmonious inter-group relations.

When used in relation to national minorities, self-determination is concerned primarily with internal jurisdiction, and does not permit the right of succession or threat to the territorial integrity of the state. The word "autonomy" is being used with greater frequency now, in this regard. While "internal self-determination" as it relates to national minorities, and "autonomy" can be regarded as functionally the same, there is no escaping the liberating connotations which continue to cling to the former term.

QUESTION: What are African-Americans? A people? A racial, ethnic or national minority?

There is no internationally agreed upon definition for either peoples or minorities. Both share many characteristics.

Also states have devised solutions in domestic law to permit nationalities to exercise varying degrees of self-determination.

While a common language, culture and religion may play an important determining role in the process of definition, the subjective factor—self-definition, the desire and ability of the group concerned to assert its will to exist as such, to be and to develop as a group, and to express its need for "autonomy" or some form of internal self-determination to achieve equal status—is a major factor in determining how a group is defined in international law.

Keeping in mind the international legal relationship between the word minority and the word victim, the most important factor calling forth legitimate demands for)internal) self-determination may be their historical circumstances, and the extent to which they have been unable or unwilling to assimilate, or have been prevented from assimilating by the majority culture, and remain trapped in a condition of permanent inequality vis-a-vis the majority.

While there has been no internationally accepted definition of national minority (let alone minority), this term continues to appear in international legal texts. Some have argued, in fact, that this is the only type of minority that truly has rights to international protection, insofar as all other are essentially immigrant or social minorities, and are covered by other human rights instruments.

While classification of African-Americans as a national minority abrogates the issue of whether they are an ethnic minority, it seems clear that their self-definition as African-Americans; their recognizability anywhere in the world as such; their distinctive music, dance, cuisine, dress and manner; and their sense of a shared history would clearly make the ethnic definition, too, and an appropriate one.

QUESTION: Do African-Americans have a unique cultural identity?

Many factors make up a people's or national minority's unique identity; these concern shared characteristics such as language, religion, or a common heritage. While most national minorities do to some degree share many of the same characteristics (as majorities, and indeed as the people of many independent states), it is important to remember that the African-American culture was consolidated under conditions of oppression. It would be difficult to argue that there is common history between the enslaved and the enslaver, i.e. a shared experience of that history, a shared interpretation of that history, or a shared evaluation of its major actors.

Assuredly, African-Americans have a unique identity. Their roots go deep into Africa, not Europe. It would be nonsensical to assume that , over the passage of generations, parents transmitted to their children nothing of the practices and understandings with which they themselves have grown up—even under the hostile conditions of enslavement, which attempted to erase all prior identities. African-American culture in the southern United States still retains many direct linkages—the basket weaving women of South Carolina, the syntax and vocabulary of the Gullah language which many have claimed provides the basis for what is commonly referred to, and coming to be taught as, African-American language, etc.

Despite the long history of theft and borrowing from African-American blues and jazz, there is nonetheless recognition of the distinctive cultural source of this music. Even today, the reference to "crossover" music asserts a continuing difference and distinctiveness of the African and Anglo-American musical cultures.

While African-Americans, like Mexicans, Cubans, French, etc., do to some degree share some of the same religious beliefs as Anglo-Americans, they also practice many religions not generally practiced by Anglo-Americans. Within the African-American community, we find, Muslins, Holly Rollers, the Green Door Society, the Yoruba, the Black Hebrews, Daddy Grace, Father Divine, and so on. The religious culture of African-American Christian churches is strikingly different from that of Anglo-American churches, to the extent that some worship an African Christ. Most African-American Christians still belong to the African Methodist Church.

QUESTION: Why does having a unique identity matter? Why can't

everybody just be the same. After all, we're all alike under the skin.

Unique cultural identities result from the historical circumstances of a people. It is not, on the collective level, what a group chooses. It results essentially from group historical experiences and situations. Therefore, the correct question in relation to minority rights law is not, why can't we all be the same—we are essentially the same—it's why should one people be oppressed because of its difference from another group? The minority rights answer is: they shouldn't, and therefore they must be afforded the rights required to be equal.

A group's ethnic identity is made up of the common experience of their families, their ancestors, and their communities. It concerns their social beliefs and religious practices, their values, their goals, their way of doing things. It means their music, their way of dress, their hair-styles, their marriage mores, their languages as well as their way of talking, their interests, their particular talents, their cooking, their dance, their sports and entertainment, their treatment of children and the elderly, and so on. These aren't attributes that people "put on," in the way that people are sometimes said to "become cultured." These are attributes that people take in with their mother's milk, from the historical practice and customs of their community. They provide the fabric for daily life.

Frequently an ethnic identity can be impoverished by oppression. Various expressions of that identity can be devalued by another ethny which has the power to enforce its values. The instance where African-American corn-row hair-styles were once rejected as unsuitable for those working in Anglo-American-controlled banks is a case in point. The denigration and suppression of an ethnic or cultural expression previously accepted as natural can only have a negative effect on inter-cultural relations.

Groups are different, and they have the right to have their differences recognized and respected as much as their sameness. These differences don't go away by ignoring them. Rather, ignoring the ethnic dimension of an individual's identity (while at the same time accepting majority ethnic identity as somehow "universal") puts minority groups at a disadvantage, since it prevents the society from being able to adequately process their unique demands, needs and requirements for equal status.

QUESTION: What if the minority doesn't express the desire to maintain its culture, but sometimes seems to be trying to escape from it and assimilate into the majority?

The fact that an oppressed minority is usually afraid to express its unique culture where an environment hostile to the culture is maintained by the state, is well understood in international law, and is the chief reason for promoting minority rights. African-Americans, like nationalities, have throughout their history affirmed a strong desire to maintain their culture in every way except where it was feared that doing so would provoke retaliation from the Anglo-Americans who controlled the apparatus of the state.

More often, the minority is simply forced to find means of accommodating the majority culture while at the same time rejecting it. In order to survive and function in situations where the majority has control and enforces its cultural preferences: in the workplace, in housing, in social services, in educational institutions, and other areas. For instances, many African-Americans provide an official and unofficial name to their children.

QUESTION: What if the individual minority member wants to assimilate, or join the dominant culture?

We should stress that it remains a feature of minority rights that the individual minority member should not be forced to avail him/herself of the rights he/she might bear as a minority individual, and should be regarded as free to assimilate into the dominant culture, if so desired, and to participate in it fully, without discrimination. However, this decision of the individual does not affect the right of the group. The individual is simply deciding to be a part of one group and not the other, or both, if the circumstances permit. Minority rights are not to be taken as enforced ghettoization of minority members.

It should be reiterated that the desirability of assimilating into the dominant culture is often simply due to the dominant culture's power in the society, and the fact that it has refused to share power with the other nationalities (minorities) and has denigrated their culture and traditions. Were the minority to achieve equal status through the exercise of minority rights, then minority traditions, values, standards of beauty, etc. would have equal appeal to that of the majority.

QUESTION: You said earlier that minority rights can mean that minorities have the right to control socio-economic and cultural institutions. Give me an example.

Let's take education. Since Brown v. Board of Education as well as during segregation, African-Americans have been integrated into the Anglo-American education system. In practice this has meant the demise, at a remarkable pace, of colleges which traditionally have served the African-American population. On the other hand, African-American students have not felt at home in Anglo-American-dominated institutions. They have not felt that these institutions adequately represented their history, their interests or their needs. In short they did not feel these institutions were "theirs," in the same way as Anglo-American students might. Many felt embarrassed by the existence of affirmative action programs, the claimed intention of which was to accelerate their entrance into the Anglo-American institutions and thereby their assimilation into Anglo-American culture, but which often were administered and interpreted in such a manner as to discredit their true capabilities or to catapult them, under intense scrutiny, into a situation of hostile and unfair competition. Applying the minority rights argument, there could be African-American and Anglo-American educational institutions as well as bi-cultural institutions. All would of course be multi-racial.

QUESTION: Does self-determination mean we could control our own school? Re-establish African-American colleges? That sounds like going back to segregation. We heard "separate but equal" before but it was never equal. Why should we believe in it now?

Yes, self-determination might entail African-American control of college curricula, programs and financing. But this wouldn't be like returning to segregation. For one thing, there would be no restrictions based on race. Those African-Americans who wished to attend Anglo-American or bi-cultural institutions would be free to do so. Anglo-Americans who wished to attend African-American or bi-cultural institutions would also be free to do so. But this time, unlike during either the segregation or the civil rights period, the control of the African-American educational situation would be in African-American hands. This would mean, among other things, that African-Americans could decide qualifications for teachers, hiring and firing, curricula, student eligibility and professional licensing standards, disciplinary codes, dress codes, fee scheduling, etc. (albeit with some restrictions resulting from mechanisms which might be put in place for ensuring parity, where required, with multicultural national standards.) However, in general African-American institutions would not be accountable to any other agency or administrative oversight outside of the African-American community.

During the period of segregation, while African-Americans did almost all the administration and teaching, African-Americans, in conjunction with the African-American community, did not establish the subjects or content, nor the priorities, nor were they culturally or politically free to promote their culture and vision of the world and the U.S. in equal-status with Anglo-Americans, or to affirm their cultural or political preferences, thus creating the intellectual and cultural ethos of their institutions. Also, during the period of segregation, African-American institutions did not have the funding to permit them to function on a par with Anglo-American institutions.

QUESTION: How would African-American colleges be in any better financial condition in a situation of self-determination?

Article 27 of the ICCPR, as amplified by Article 1 of the Declaration on the Rights of Persons Belonging to National or Ethnic, Religious and Linguistic Minorities, requires governments to "create conditions" favorable to the preservation and development of minority cultures. In practice this has often meant giving minorities jurisdiction over their own schools. The educational sector has historically been the most common sector for minorities to exercise their cultural rights. The funding of these educational institutions has been a government responsibility, financed by a share of public moneys, i.e. transfer payments in those situations where minorities were not also given the right to raise money in the numerous ways that governments do: by power to tax, by licensing fees, etc. (See, for instance, Articles 41-43 of the Statute of Autonomy of the Basque Country, 1979, in Appendix I.) In Canada, the federal structure and provincial taxation rights thereunder has permitted French Canadians, by means of their control of the Quebec provincial government, to directly control a sector of the taxation rights accorded to Quebec and secure funding for education institutions and the Desjardin banking movement.

QUESTION: If African-Americans controlled their own educational system, how would this make a difference?

First of all, it would enable African-Americans both to preserve and develop their unique cultural identities by accepting community practices and understandings as normative rather than (at best) "different but all right." On the higher level, this is not just a matter of teaching African-American literature or studying African art. It also permits the expression of an African-American perspective on all the various disciplines: history, political science, law, sociology, psychology, economics, anthropology, and so on—in the same way that this naturally occurs in, say, Canadian, Quebecois, French, and British educational institutions. It creates responsiveness not just to the needs but also to the views and practices of the African-American community, seeking to affirm, substantiate and empower these views (both intellectually and in actuality). As such, it would serve as a cornerstone and pillar establishing and ensuring the unique African-American intellectual contribution to global scholarship.

Secondly, it would mean jobs for the community—not just jobs in the present (teaching and administrative positions) but also the guarantee of jobs in the future, for the students coming up, since education as well as professional and other licensing authority could be geared towards meeting community needs.

QUESTION: Since "integration" and the significant movements of whites into traditionally black schools and colleges, many African-Americans have wanted to set up schools to preserve their own culture. But then they thought: what was the use in establishing schools, if non-discrimination meant they were obliged to open their doors to whites, who might come in and take over. Could they have a policy saying no whites were allowed to come?

It isn't a matter of the presence of the whites or any other race, it's a matter of establishing the purpose and curricula of the school in relation to the highest African-American standards and needs. All people should be invited to assist a worthwhile purpose. The curricula and policies would be dominated by universal values as understood by the African-American community, as well as courses specifically geared to meet the needs of the African-American community.

QUESTION: Does African-American control of the educational system mean that kids would be learning Afrocentrism?

What African-American control of African-American education means is just that: control of schools by the African-American community. It's not simply a question of the curriculum, it's a question of the administration, philosophy, world view, etc. it will be the democratic consensus of the community which decides those qualified to determine what goes into the African-American curriculum.

African culture inhabits African-American culture like the sap, the tree. Whether consciously rediscovered, or simply passed on as family practice from one generation to the next it is pervasive throughout African-Americans' daily habits, ways of thought and belief, modes of relating, political and lifestyle preferences, and so on. For generations it has represented their heritage and their aspirations. There is no way for the two to be torn apart. And yet, with the centuries of life in America, the African-Americans have evolved to become a new

African people in North America—Africans who are also American, and whose relation with Europe is significantly different from that of African or Asian populations. Who is to say how that identity, given its freedom to develop according to its own tastes and abilities, might evolve?

If the African-American community as a whole wants Afrocentrism, then likely it would play a larger role. But there are other elements in the community as well, wanting other things. Undoubtedly Afrocentrism represents yet another rich channel of African culture pouring into the African-American pot. But insofar as Afrocentrism is (self)-consciously imported, insofar as it can be sensed as representing something other than what the people presently are, then it must be recognized as being a part, not the whole of the African-American culture; as feeding into the hole, enriching it, undoubtedly, but not being it. The whole is what the African-American people are, today, as they stand, as they remember, as they have forgotten, as they experience subliminally, habitually, and so on. As UNESCO's World Conference on Cultural Policies in Mexico recently declared:

> [Culture] comprises the whole complex of distinctive spiritual material, intellectual and emotional features that characterize a society or social group. It includes not only the arts and letters, but also modes of life, the fundamental rights of the human being, value systems, traditions and beliefs.

It would be a mistake to assume that African-American control of their own schools would mean that they would have to go out and start behaving in a way that they were not presently behaving. Unless they wanted to do so. Unless they decided, as a group, to do so. It would e similar to taking all the noteworthy English writers, poets, scholars, musicians and exponents of "high culture," as comprising the whole of English culture. Where, then, would one find steak and kidney bean pie? Or stiff upper lips?

QUESTION: What could self-determination mean in relation to other jurisdictions such as criminal justice?

It's well known that the United States has the highest incarceration rate in the world in relation to its African-American population—in fact, four times the rate of white dominated South Africa. Much of African-Americans' disproportionately higher rates of incarceration stem not only from acts deriving from circumstances of poverty and oppression that they endure, but also from the disproportionate tendency of law enforcement to apprehend, convict, harass, intimidate and scapegoat the African-American community. Much also stems from the exacerbated tensions between law enforcement and enforcement personnel has been a largely unsuccessful attempt to mitigate the poor relations existing between the African-American community and the criminal justice system insofar as such black personnel have not themselves been in control of their working environment, but rather caught up in it like helpless cogs in a machine, forced rather to prove themselves to their environment (the various peer groups and hierarchies within the criminal justice system) than to their community.

Dr. Roberta Sykes, an eloquent spokeswoman for the Black Aboriginal minority of Australia, made the following observation pertinent to police work in her own community, which suffers similarly high rates of incarceration:

> We have to work out methods whereby Blacks can have immediate and profound influence in policy and practice. It is my contention that it does not matter very much what color a police officer is—what matters is who he or she is accountable to.

If African-Americans were enabled to influence the criminal justice system or establish their own criminal justice system insofar as it concerned the African-American community—not just through personnel, hiring, firing and appointments, but through a systematized form of African-American input into criminal law content, policy, behavior codes, sentencing, parole, passage or prioritizing of laws, etc., it is likely that an entirely new relationship between the African-American communities and law enforcement would be achieved. Law enforcement would be seen as it properly should be—as an extension of the community values, needs and understandings, and responsible to it rather than to politicians, absentee property holders or Anglo-American philosophic, socio-economic and political priorities or public opinion. The community would have the freedom to find alternatives to incarceration; to give appropriate consideration to community evaluations to offenders; to give due weight to mitigating socio-economic and cultural factors in relation to crimes and misdemeanors; and to stop harassment by establishing procedures to ensure enforcement responsiveness and responsibility to the community and community evaluation of service and service personnel.

QUESTION: If we want to talk about the African-American community

controlling its education and criminal justice systems, etc., don't we have to talk about how we decide what the African-American community wants?

Yes, African-Americans will need to institutionalize a political and democratic means of accessing African-American demands and needs. The main question African-Americans need to politically and democratically determine is whether, as a people, they wish to assimilate, or to be empowered, collectively. Their answer to this question determines the direction that they should follow—civil rights or minority rights.

This could be done by holding some form of referendum for African-American voters only, which might draw on the good offices of the United Nations to provide the required expertise and legitimacy. There are numerous bodies in the international world concerned with the establishment of electoral procedures under a wide variety of circumstances; they would have answers to the numerous technical questions which would arise in that regard. The required expertise is there, if there is the will and desire to access it.

Also, African-Americans need establish democratic structures or institutions which will provide arenas for policy debates, and the emergence of an African-American-elected leadership responsible to the African-American people.

This may mean establishing a national Council, and African-American Congress, and African-American Assembly or whatever, and demanding its recognition by the government as the only legitimate voice of the African-American people.

QUESTION: What are the advantages of an African-American National Council, Assembly, Congress, or what have you?

It would enable African-Americans to choose their own leadership, which would have to answer first to them. This would encourage the leadership to put forward policies that African-Americans want and need that reflect their history and circumstances. This is particularly important when the federal government puts into place policies that solely or even predominantly affect African-Americans. Rather than consulting with people whom the federal government has decided it is willing to recognize as African-American leaders, the federal government would be encouraged to confer with a body which is directly responsible to the African-American people, and hence responsive to its needs. Because the National Council, etc., would have been democratically chosen by the African-American people and legal recognized as the sole voice of African-Americans, the federal government will be less inclined to behave as if this leadership may or may not (depending on federal government whim or interest) represent the true will of the African-American people. It would be unlike the present situation where individual leaders are summoned for consultation to the White House, and remain just that: individual VIPs—any one whom might be "de-legitimized" simply by failing to receive an invitation next time.

The National Council, or whatever, would provide an apparatus for the African-American people which would enable them to make decisions and institute planning in relation to African-American philosophy and cultural paradigms as it relates to how they see the best interest, globally as well as nationally.

Further, this authorized representation would counter the present situation where media heroes engage with world leaders on whatever issues may move them (or be mediagenic at the time), representing the authority of the African-American people without having been legitimately given it.

A National Council, once integrated within the governmental structures of the American politico-legal system, would be able to function like another layer of government, regulating and responding to its key population group within the spheres of its own jurisdictions.

QUESTION: What kind of politico-legal system can offer African-Americans these jurisdictions, bearing in mind that the African-American population is not concentrated in one area, but rather is spread out through many states?

True, the African-American population is spread out, but that may prove to be advantageous. For one thing, territorial concentration has a tendency to give rise to movements which seek to establish self-determination through taking over a specific territory, and demanding political independence. This is threatening to both the state and the local non-minority population which may be located within such territories, insofar as it may arouse fears of secession, and dismemberment of the country. No state easily countenances secession, and in any event, African-Americans may not have the relative numbers, power, or desire to move toward taking political control of a specific territory, so long as their survival needs can be better obtained as an integrated part of the country they feel they helped to build.

The international legal norm of minority rights instead suggests the establishment of politico-legal structures within the framework of the state, related specifically to the use and needs of African-Americans as a dispersed minority. While in practice and in law, territorially-concentrated minorities' needs are more easily facilitated, there are existing and historical precedents for empowering dispersed minorities which could serve as examples for African-Americans. This does not preclude the combination of local territorially-based autonomies with a national politico-legal structure geared towards a dispersed population.

Insofar as each minority situation has its own particular conditions and is advanced or constrained, according to the needs, structures and views of the state with which it is negotiating implementation of its rights, it is unlikely that the model of any other country would be adopted in the United States without substantial reversion or embellishment. What is needed at this point is to use these historical models as a means of initiating a discussion of new possibilities.

QUESTION: How would African-Americans go about establishing a National Council?

What is most necessary is widespread recognition of the need and consequent demand for such a body within the community itself. Ideally, at such time, a non-partisan entity permitting all groups, large and small, to participate, might serve the technical role of establishing he procedures and facilitating the process. While the UN might assist such an entity, and legitimize and provide expertise to the process, insofar as the process must be sufficiently self-developed, the UN, international organizations and African states must plainly see a manifestation of the demand before participating.

QUESTION: What role would the United States government play?

Since any such National Council, Assembly, or what have you, formed at the initiative of the African-American community and suing for government recognition, affects traditional power relations in the state, its recognition could entail constitutional and/or legal changes, bureaucratic changes, changes in the tax structures or transfer payments, according to the powers which might be acceded to it and/or, attendantly, to the African-American community.

At the present time, the United States government has no single, logical, constitutionally-delineated and institutionally-coordinated policy for dealing with its national minorities. Indeed, with the emergence of "rainbows" and "multiculturalism" even within African-American activist organizations themselves, and the failure of the major political parties to raise, let alone deal with, African-American issues, there appears to be desire, within both the white and black echelons of power, for the existence and problems of African-Americans to be submerged in the generalized distress of what has been termed the American "underclass."

And yet, time is running out. African-American populations dominate major metropolitan areas. Already the decay in American cities is ominous. Something has to be done, of the good ship U.S.A., punctured by the gaping holes that are its major cities, and ravaged by a major ethnic conflict that could approach third world proportions, will sink. It is in the interest of the country as a whole to solve the problem of African-American inequality. African-American autonomy—which may indeed by the only way this community will be able to develop, insofar as four decades of civil rights have produced neither assimilation nor non-discrimination—is therefore ultimately in the interest of the USA.

Consider the similar situation of majoritarian democracy in South Africa. Will the present South Africa under majority rule be able to satisfy the desire of the Zulu—and indeed, the Afrikaner minority—for protection and maintenance of their unique cultures? Already these groups are demanding minority rights and internal self-determination. If such internationally-recognized rights are not, to some degree, accorded to them, will South Africa be able to achieve the peace required for its economic development?

QUESTION: Why should African-Americans give much value to achieving true democratic participation through democratic pluralism? In most democracies where elections are in place, people can't even be bothered to vote.

The simple attainment of democracy as it concerns African-Americans and as it is reflected in some form of a national council permitting the formulation of policy and election of leaders directly responsible to the African-American community, in and of itself represents an assertion of the right of the African-American community to existence and to socio-economic development as such. It represents a mechanism for encouraging the direction of political power and economic resources into the community. Even should the voting pattern of African-Americans in elections that concerned their community alone subsequently reflect an indifference similar to that of other communities, this would not change the immense impact the very existence of such politico-legal and socio-economic institutions would have in promoting African-American equal-status relations through creating a high degree of political and economic interdependence in place of dependence with the majority community.

QUESTION: Will it be necessary to wage a war of liberation in order for African-Americans to achieve minority rights?

This may not necessary. We have before us the example of the restructuring of eastern Europe, where systemic changes too vast to have been contemplated even a year earlier, once initiated, took place swiftly and with little bloodshed.

Why? Because the time of these ideas had come. The old order was helpless before them. The agreement on the need for change was general and all-pervasive, and therefore unstoppable. In the case of America, it is clear that the explosive situation caused by the systemically-enforced inequality of African-Americans is reaching the end of its containment. That something must be done—something new—will become apparent to most. Once this realization becomes pervasive, sufficient numbers of the decision-makers in all communities will be enabled to facilitate the systemic shift to minority rights required to avoid catastrophe.

QUESTION: If self-determination for African-Americans is so beneficial, what can possibly hold it back?

The major questions remain the extent to which the African-American struggle will meet with the good will of the United States ruling circles, and how prepared they are to make sacrifices. The economic capability for it exists in the U.S.—inherent at minimum in the redirection of economic resources already being spent on containment of African-Americans in situations of political and social malaise. The international paradigms re there—paradigms which need not be taken as gospel, but simply as a way of introducing conceptual flexibility, of freeing the mind from the rigidities of past practice and opening up new possibilities.

Again, as Dr. Roberta Sykes noted with regard to her own Black Aboriginal community in Australia:

> Being supportive of self-determination is attitudinal and behavior, so there is no handbook or set of commandments to make the task easier. At each point along the way, policy makers must ensure that their work is guided by determinations made in the Black community about the Black community's welfare. Anything less is not self-determination, and the principle of self-determination is non-negotiable.

America stands in danger of running aground on its minority problem. If good will cannot be generated from traditional American moral values—the belief in equality, fairness, sharing and justice—then in the end it may come to be realized, willy-nilly, through another no less quintessential American belief—that of enlightened and pragmatic self interest.

ENDNOTES:

1 While the UN Sub-Commission was unable to achieve a consensus on the definition of minority prepared at its request by Mr. Jules Deschênes, his definition suffices for this article: "A group of citizens of a State, constituting a numerical minority and in a non-dominant position in that State, endowed with ethnic, religious or linguistic characteristics which differ from those of the majority of the population, having a sense of solidarity with one another. motivated, if only implicitly, by a collective will to survive and whose aim is to achieve equality witthe majority in fact and in law." UN Doc. E/CN.4/Sub.2/1985/Para. 181.

2 UNPO Monitor: Draft Summary of the Principle Points Raised at the United Nations Working Group on Indigenous Populations. Day 2. Morning Session. Tuesday. July 25, 1994.

3 Y.N. Kly, The Ana-Social Contract 1987.

4 IHRAAM submitted a lengthy Communication to the Human Rights Committee, August 9th. 1993.

5 Cited in Francesco Capotorti, Study on the Rights of Persons Belonging to Ethnic. Religious and Linguistic Minorities. United Nations. 1979, p. 8.

6 Richard L. Engstrom and Michael D. Mcdonald, "The Effect of At-Large Versus District Elections on Racial Representation in U.S. Municipalities," in Bernard Grofmann and Arend Lijphart, eds. Electoral Laws and Their Political Consequences. 1986, p. 116.

7 Cynthia H. Enloe. "Internal Colonialism, Federalism and Alternative State Development Strategies," Publlus: The Journal of Federalism, Vol. vii, Fall 1977. p. 150.

8 Derrick Bell. Race, Racism and American Law. 1969.

9 An analysis of the current U .S. judicial response to discrimination is provided in *A Popular Guide to Minority Rights*, in the article "Non-Discrimination in U.S. Courts: A Non-Solution?" by Aviam Soifer.

10 See Kenneth McRae, Conflict and Compromise In Multilingual Societies: Switzerland, 1983.

11 See Eric A. Nordlinger. Conflict Regulation In Divided Societies, Occasional Papers in International Affairs, Harvard University, January 1972.

12 Ian Brownlie, "The Rights of Peoples in Modern International Law," in James Crawford, ed.. The Rights of Peoples, 1988, p. 5-6.

13 See keynote address, "African-Americans and the Right to Self-Determination," Proceedings of the Hamline Conference on African-Americans and the Rights to Self-Determination, herein.

14 For an indication of the continuing importance of this view, see Final Report of the Martin Ennals Symposium on Self-Determination, March 4-6, 1993. International Alert. London. 1993.

15 See submission by the French government, drafting process of the Declaration on Minorities.

16 See Lorenzo Turner, Africanisms In the Gullah Dialect, 1969 reproduction of 1949 edition.

17 See UNESCO, Final Report of the World Conference on Cultural Policies. Mexico City. 26 July-6 August 1982, p. 41.

18 Cited in Francesco Capotorti, supra, note 5. p. 8. The Yugoslav Government stated that it "wishes to underscore its conviction that the so-called 'subjective factor' is in many aspects dependent on the political stereotypes and the cultural and social circumstances prevailing in the individual social communities in which the members of minorities live and work. Historical experiences have shown that the 'indifference' of the members of minorities towards their national origin, position and rights are, as a rule, the consequence of the social and other circumstances in which they live. In societies with a prevailing negative attitude of the 'majority' towards the 'minority,' the members of the minorities are fearful that any declaration of one's national, ethnic, cultural and other characteristics might be interpreted as a so-called 'civil disloyalty' on the part of the minority concerned. Therefore, it would be inappropriate to ascribe too much importance to the need of a "declaration of desire" by the members of any minority in order to preserve their own national, ethnic, cultural and other features, and to manifest their awareness of their affiliation to a particular minority, especially in the case of a minority which has for decades been subjected to the pressures of systematic assimilation and de-nationalization."

19 See B.T. Warington's Five Finger, One Hand Solution.

20 See Article 3 of the UN Declaration on Minorities.

21 Serena L. Swaggers and H. Larry Winecoff, "Changing Profiles of Black Institutions of Higher Learning: A Study of Fourteen Private. Historically Black Institutions in the Southeast," as cited in IHRAAM Newsletter. Vol. 2. No. 3.

22 See Andrew Hacker, Two Nations: Black and White, Separate, Hostile, Unequal, 1992.

23 The Permanent Court of International Justice rendered an advi¬sory opinion affirming this right as early as 1935. See Advisory Opinion of 6 April 1935 on Minority Schools In Albania, P.C.I.J., Ser. A/B, No. 64, 17.

24 Quoted by Anders Arfwedson, Introduction to Information Kit on the 1994 Decade Theme: "Culture and Development," Paris, UNESCO, 1994.

25 "U.S. Imprisons Black Men at 4 Times S. Africa's Rate." Los Angeles Times, January 3. 1991.

26 Roberta B. Sykes. "Self-Determination: Implications for Criminal Justice Policy Makers." Kayleen M. Hazlehurst, ed.. Justice Programs for Aboriginal and Other Indigenous Communities, Australian Institute of Criminology. Seminar Proceedings. No. 7, p. 25.

27 In this instance, reference is made to cases where offenders seeking

parole (or indeed, being tried) are unable to benefit from the high standing they may enjoy within their community, as attested to by their local religious, educational or other community leaders, insofar as this testimony is not given the credence which might adhere to similar testimony given by a body of Anglo-American community figures.

28 See Y.N. Kly, International Law and the Black Minority in the U.S., 1990 (third edition).

29 See Sykes, supra, note 14, p. 28.

Made in the USA
Middletown, DE
27 January 2021

32536603R00116